MacLaboratory
for
Psychology

Student Laboratory Manual

THIRD EDITION

MacLaboratory for Psychology

THIRD EDITION

Student Laboratory Manual

Douglas L. Chute
DREXEL UNIVERSITY

Robert S. Daniel
UNIVERSITY OF MISSOURI

Brooks/Cole Publishing Company
Pacific Grove, California

ITP™
The trademark ITP is used under license.

Brooks/Cole Publishing Company
A Division of Wadsworth, Inc.

© 1994 by Wadsworth, Inc., Belmont, California 94002. All rights reserved. No part of this book may be reproduced, stored in a retrieval system, or transcribed, in any form or by any means—electronic, mechanical, photocopying, recording, or otherwise—without the prior written permission of the publisher, Brooks/Cole Publishing Company, Pacific Grove, California 93950, a division of Wadsworth, Inc.

Printed in the United States of America
10 9 8 7 6 5 4 3 2 1

ISBN 0-534-23198-5

Sponsoring Editor: *Marianne Taflinger*
Marketing Representatives: *Rita Ferrandino and Ron Shelly*
Editorial Assistant: *Virge Pirelli-Minetti*
Production Coordinator: *Marlene Thom*
Production Assistant: *Tessa A. McGlasson*
Manuscript Editor: *Carol Dondrea*
Cover Design: *Katherine Minerva*
Typesetting: *Anker Publishing Company, Inc.*
Printing and Binding: *Malloy Lithographing, Inc.*

Apple, the Apple logo, AppleLink, AppleShare, HyperCard, QuickTime, ResEdit, PowerPC, Performa, and Macintosh are registered trademarks of Apple Computer, Inc. Maelstrom is a trademark of Ambrosia Software. Sniffy is a trademark of the Governing Council of the University of Toronto. Excel is a registered trademark of Microsoft Corporation. LabDriver is a registered trademark of National Instruments, Inc. Reference to these or other products is for informational purposes only and no endorsement or recommendation is implied.

MacLaboratory and MacLaboratory software, including all code, scripts, icons, text and resources, are Copyright © 1984, 1985, 1986, 1987, 1988, 1989, 1990, 1992, 1993, 1994 by Douglas L. Chute and/or MacLaboratory, Inc. Use of these products is permitted only under the terms of your specific licensing agreement.

ACKNOWLEDGMENTS

MacLaboratory for Psychology is more than just a student's laboratory manual, a collection of faculty research tools, or some multimedia software. It is a "living curriculum" pioneered by my mentor Robert S. Daniel some 40 or more years ago. In subsequent iterations, *MacLaboratory for Psychology* has persisted and is currently used by thousands of students annually worldwide. It may not be the most popular at the time a student takes the course, but it often ranks highest of all courses in retrospect, after graduation. I believe this is because our curriculum offers the student a true scientific experience as well as a dose of hard work. At the time, many students don't really want such an experience—after all, comparatively few are psychology, or even science, majors. Nevertheless, there is something special about the process approach and the challenge to students to create their own scientific logic. They eventually discover they have learned critical thinking skills (even if they circumvented some of the harder requirements) and this logic can be useful in whatever their chosen careers. I have taken to calling this process "media mentoring" because the phrase conveys a level of ambiguity about who is teaching whom. This is as it should be.

As a teacher, I have been impressed by my colleagues at other universities, colleges, and high schools who have found unique and creative ways to adapt the materials for their students needs. The computer has really made this possible although I don't know if it has actually made anything easier. I think not. What the computer has allowed us to do is teach different things from those we were able to teach before. I am grateful to my colleagues and all the users who have offered fresh and invigorating ideas. I trust that software will allow this process to continue and that networks will facilitate our mutually beneficial exchanges.

In many of the universities licensing *MacLaboratory*, graduate students actually run the laboratory classes. When I was doing the same thing for Dr. Daniel 25 years ago, I was the embodiment of the adage that "you never know anything 'till you try and teach it." Graduate students still find this to be true as they learn the subtleties and intricacies of this curriculum. We have always viewed our role as an integral part of graduate student training.

There is a tendency to think of academic software as just another form of the textbook. This is quite untrue in many respects. For example, we have had many publishers over the years, but through brand loyalty, service, and user dedication, we endure. By building on the past and making a long-term commitment our work becomes more valuable. We have concentrated on the value added by productivity tools, and tended to eschew the simply tutorial. We have never been remaindered. Perhaps the most important difference is the number of experts required for the creation, distribution, support, and production of a comprehensive curriculum solution. For historical reasons alone, I am accorded more credit than is my due. I have simply been the steward of this "living curriculum" that grows and evolves almost on its own.

Of the many people who have been essential to the success of this curriculum, I will name a few so you can appreciate the magnitude and scope of their efforts. Each has been a part of our collective success and I thank them for their contributions. *MacLaboratory* in its computerized form is now 10 years old. One of the hardest parts to maintain over such a span of time is enthusiasm and motivation. Thus, I would like to especially acknowledge Bob Westall, our Senior Product Manager. Also in the "longevity category" are Jim Anker; Joe Barisa; Bob Bliss; Jesse, Deborah, and Andrew Chute; John Harvey; Leon Hirsch; Melanie Hoag; Morrell Jacobs; and Scott Quillen. I am also especially grateful to Ryan Sandridge who has risen rapidly through the ranks and so ably took over as our HyperCard Product Manager. Past programmers whose code still lives on include Dave Barosso, Derek White, and, yes, even Bill Knott. Our total software effort is about 600,000 lines of code and 1.5 gigabytes of other resources for psychology.

MacLaboratory's "person of the decade" is Margaret Bliss, who created our operations environment. Here she is pictured basking in the emissions of some Apple prototype hardware of a few

Acknowledgments vii

years ago. This was one of the first "color" images captured in the days when we still taught class with 128K Macintoshes.

In the category of advice, support, a shoulder to lean on, and generosity of spirit, I particularly thank Rick Breslin, Denny Brown, Tom Canavan, John Collins, John Noon, Nadine Perkey, Rich Schneider, and Darryl Weiner. Major contributions have come from Drexel University; Apple Computer, Inc.; the Pew Charitable Trusts; and the Hanspeter Albisser Stiftung. In earlier days, the award money from our EDUCOM prizes was all that kept things going.

Colleagues, graduate students, and teachers who have directly affected my work in the various and oft-times subtle ways such things happen include Regula Bäggli, Barry Bank, Ed Barnoski, Rich Berg, Ray Brebach, John Castellan, John Flynn, Russ Geen, Tony Glascock, Jeff Graham, Tom Hewett, Don Kausler, Les Krames, Dave MacDonald, Lauren Montenegro, John Mueller, Pauline Nye, Ed O'Brien, Banu Onaral, Denise Parks, Terry Shaw, Cindy Socha, Mary Spiers, John Villiger, Toni Welch, Dennis Wright, Donna Yaure, and Eric Zillmer. I cannot express sufficient gratitude to Bob Daniel, the founder of the journal *Teaching of Psychology*, and to this curriculum.

I would like to thank the staffs of the Psychology Department and Neuropsychology Graduate Program at Drexel University and the staff of the Office of Computing Services for managing the day-to-day problems of the 1300 students a year that take the course locally and serve as our testing and teaching resource. The curriculum simply could not be delivered without their constant attention and good will.

I have come to learn a bit about the publishing industry, and I must express my gratitude and admiration, especially for their foresight, to Bill Roberts, Marianne Taflinger, and the talented and hard-working people at Brooks/Cole. *MacLaboratory* presents new challenges and long-term consequences as publishing moves from a book industry to an information industry. I am confident that the support, sales, marketing, and technology groups of Wadsworth and Brooks/Cole will be in your service as an integral part of the "living curriculum."

CONTENTS

READ ME FIRST	1	Quick Start
EXPERIMENTAL METHODS	11	Introduction
	17	Measuring Extrasensory Perception
	29	Measuring Motor Learning
	45	Principles of Statistical Inference
	61	Optimizing Skill Acquisition
	77	Proposing Your Own Research
BEHAVIORAL NEUROSCIENCES	91	Introduction
	97	The Brain: Structure and Function
	105	Measuring Hemispheric Specialization
COGNITIVE SCIENCES	117	Introduction
	121	Measuring Short-Term Memory
	133	How Fast Do You Think?
	153	Are Two Heads Better Than One?
	169	Manipulating Mental Images
	183	Neural Modeling in Visual Perception
LEARNING AND CONDITIONING	189	Introduction
	193	Operant Conditioning of the Rat
	223	Classical Conditioning of Emotion
SENSATION AND PERCEPTION	233	Introduction
	239	Discovering the Lies Told by Your Eyes
	249	Just How Well Do You Hear?

PERSONALITY AND SOCIAL PSYCHOLOGY	257	Introduction
	261	Subliminal Psychodynamic Activation
	275	Is There a Nazi Personality?
	283	Measuring Personality: Type A or B
	295	How Do You Conduct a Good Survey?
INDIVIDUAL RESEARCH PROJECT	307	Conclusion
	309	Design, Create, Conduct, Analyze, and Present Your Own Research

QUICK START

READ ME FIRST

The program *MacLaboratory for Psychology* contains both teaching components and authentic research-grade capabilities. Essentially, you can have a sophisticated psychology laboratory on your hard drive, CD-ROM, or over a network, depending on how your Macintosh, Performa, or PowerPC is set up.

In this Quick Start section we describe the basic interface for the software so you can get up and running right away. There is both good news and bad news in this basic "quickie" approach. The good news is that you readily learn how to navigate through the HyperCard teaching stacks as well as learn the general operation of the *MacLaboratory* research applications. The bad news is that you might overlook the challenges and opportunities provided by the software, which allows you to design and conduct real, millisecond-accurate research in such areas as clinical evaluation, motivation, emotion, human cognition, perception, motor performance, neuropsychology, social attitudes, learning, or other areas of interest to the science of psychology. To acquire this higher level of proficiency, you have to work through the documentation that accompanies the software and through the various tutorials and examples that are supplied. Although this may seem daunting just now, you will find that you don't have to have any specialized computer or programming skills to be able to conduct research that is as sophisticated as that in the professional journals. In any case, let's avoid the bad news for a while and explore some features of the software.

Working with *MacLaboratory* is not something you want to do by yourself, in the dead of night. The teaching and learning strategies contained in this Lab Manual work best with a partner or other collaborators, along with the guidance of your instructor.

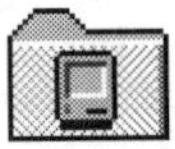

BASIC REQUIREMENTS: SYSTEM

We assume you have a basic familiarity with your Macintosh or one of its compatibles and know how to plug in the CD-ROM disk or load the appropriate floppies onto your hard disk drive. You can launch an application, experiment file, or HyperCard stack by clicking in the usual way. If this sounds unfamiliar, you should ask someone or go over the "getting started" materials that came with your machine. Don't be afraid to experiment—it's actually very difficult to damage the hardware or the software without resorting to a flame thrower, drenching it with Pepsi, or applying other extreme measures! Perhaps your Macintosh has already been set up as described in the *MacLaboratory for Psychology* documentation that comes with the software.

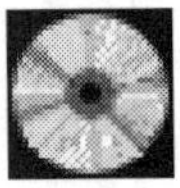

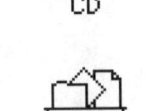

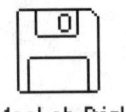

To get the most from *MacLaboratory*'s capabilities, you should have at least 5 megabytes of RAM, a color monitor, HyperCard, and System 7 with QuickTime. A spreadsheet such as Excel is convenient for data analysis, but not necessary. If your machine does not have color or some other feature, there is still a lot you can accomplish, except, perhaps, in color perception! Consult the documentation for suggestions and setup for System 6.x or black-and-white machines. The CD-ROM version of *MacLaboratory for Psychology* contains a number of larger QuickTime movies, additional software, and an enhanced multimedia format that are not available by floppy distribution. It is best to have a fast CD player or access across a network so you can download folders to your hard drive. *MacLaboratory* can run over a network, but speed and timing accuracy will be variable.

BASIC NAVIGATION: STACKS

Locate the Perception Folder in your software. Open the stack "Visual Perception" for an example of how to navigate around the HyperCard part of your software. The stacks are primarily used as teaching tools to present relevant psychological information. You may also use them to launch various illustrative experiments as outlined in this Lab Manual.

Every *MacLaboratory* stack uses the same Navigation Palette and interface. The Introduction Card presents a representative graphic and some text explaining its general purpose.

Read Me First

If you have followed along this far, click on the Map button to see an overview of the contents in the stack.

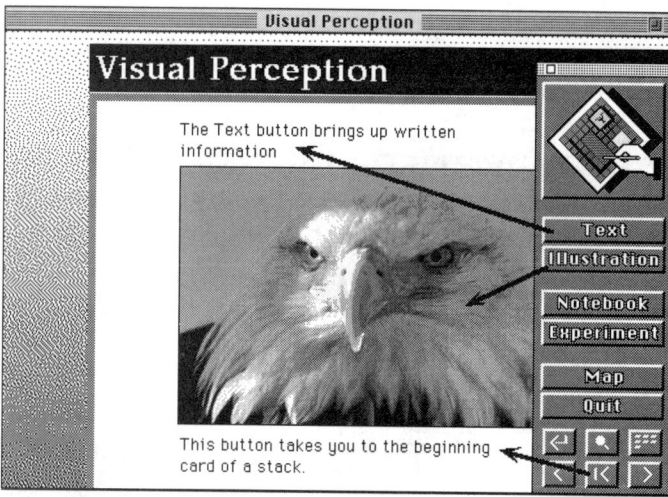

Each stack is divided into two main sections. The Notebook section provides illustrations or movies and text on important content areas.

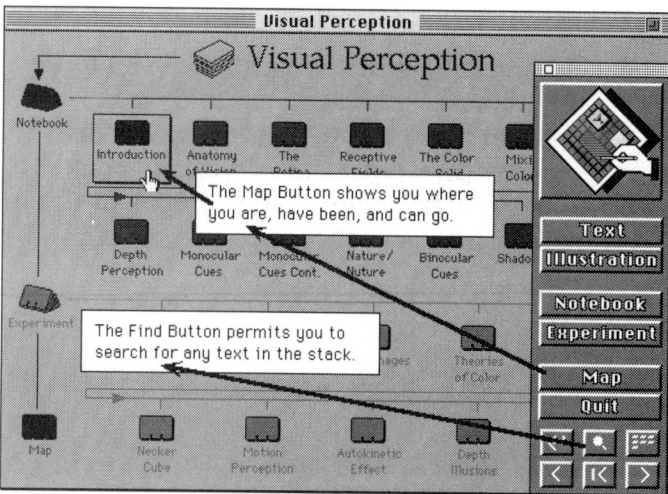

The Experiment section includes information on the setting up and running of experimental protocols. In many cases an Experiment File created by one of the research applications will be launched. Although it is not necessary to use these HyperCard "front ends" to run experiments, they can be a useful way to present easily edited instructions.

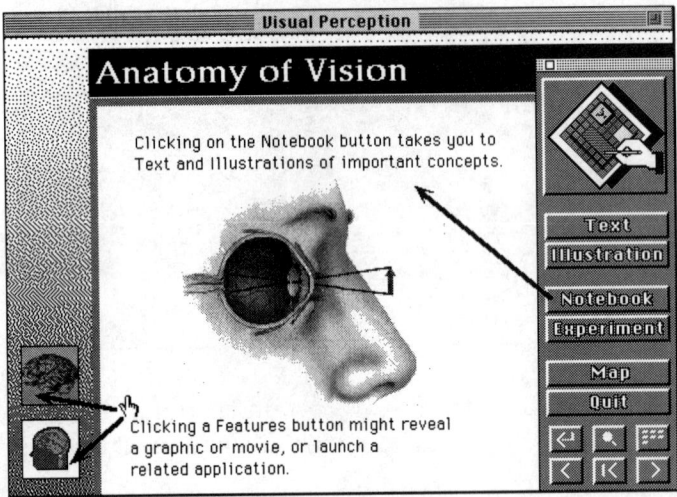

If you are still following along with the Visual Perception stack, click the Experiment button. This takes you to the Experiment section and in this case brings up a color patch. Change the monitor's contrast and/or brightness settings all the way down. What happens to the appearance of the different colors? Can you develop a hypothesis about why many municipalities are now ordering yellow instead of red fire engines?

Read Me First 5

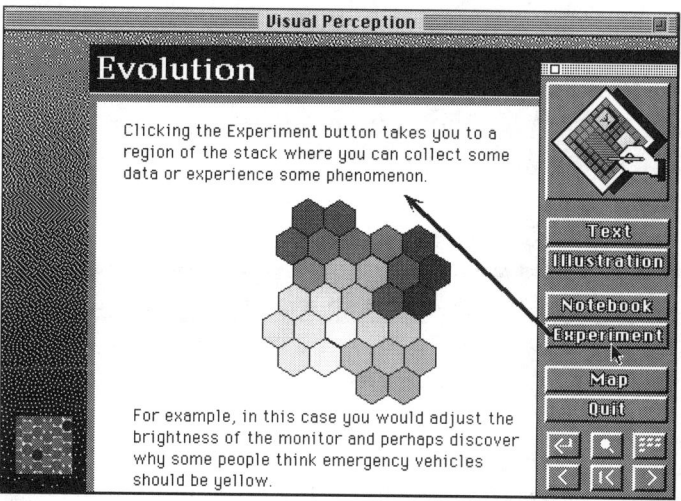

Feel free to explore around the stack. There are some optical illusions and other visual phenomena that you might find interesting. You might also get the feeling that you are more than a little lost. Aside from the Map, other navigation buttons can help you keep your bearings. The Go Back button retraces your path. The Find button searches for any matching text you have entered. The Recent button shows you all the cards you have recently visited. You can click on any one in the dialog box and immediately jump there.

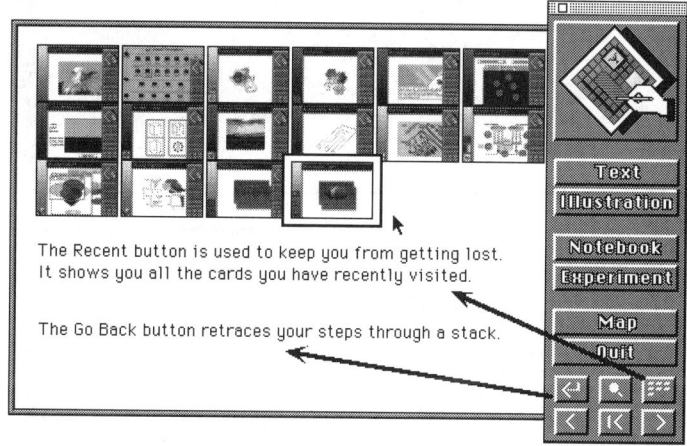

If you have difficulty launching HyperCard, you may not have enough memory assigned to the application. This is a common problem. To fix it choose the application at the Finder level and select Get Info under the File menu. You can then set the preferred size in the dialog box.

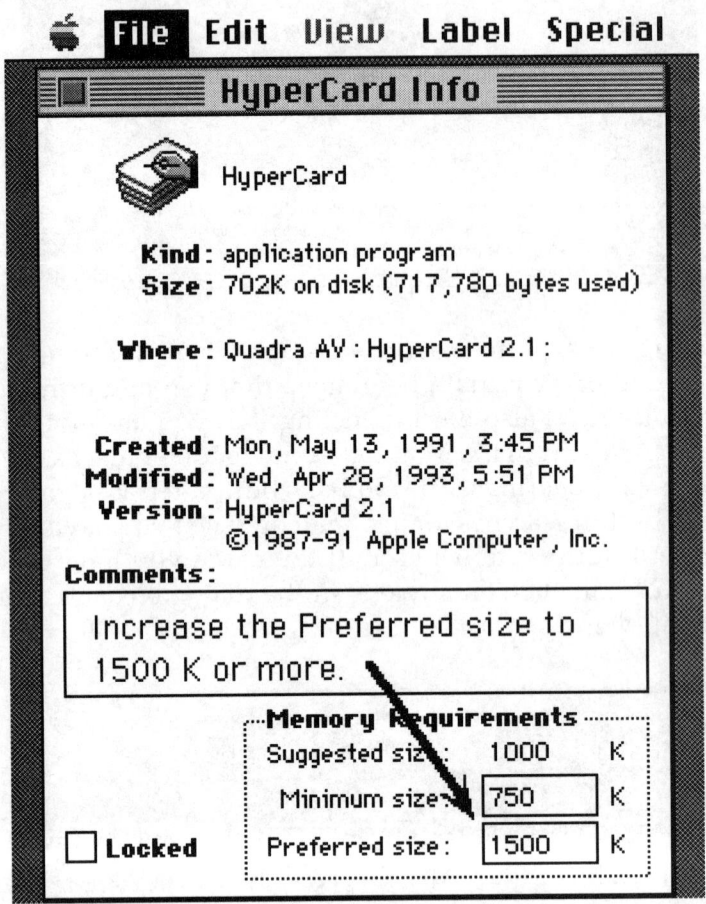

BASIC OPERATIONS: APPLICATIONS

The *MacLaboratory* package has a number of specialized standalone applications that allow you to create and edit your own research designs. This research software is located in the Applications Folder or the Utilities Folder of *MacLaboratory*. Editing is not covered in this Quick Start section. You will have to refer to *MacLaboratory* documentation, which is also available from

Read Me First

Brooks/Cole Publishing Company. (Brooks/Cole can be contacted at 1-800-354-9706.)

When an experiment has been edited, say in the application Reaction Time, a file is created that contains all the information necessary for accurate presentation of stimuli and collection of responses. As an example, we will run a file called Decision Time that is used for an experiment later in this Manual. Locate the Cognition Folder; within it, you will find an Experiment Files folder. Open the Reaction Time experiment file, Decision Time, by double-clicking it.

Reaction Time

You will collect some left-handed and some right-handed **simple reaction time** data, as well as some **choice reaction time** data, where you don't know which hand you will be asked to use. Then look at your personal performance for each hand. Do you think your preferred hand is faster than your nonpreferred hand? If you have the spreadsheet Excel available, you can run the Decision Time Excel Macro located in the Excel Data Templates Folder to automatically tabulate and graph your data.

Experiment Files

By the way, you might have noticed that **simple reaction time** is written in bold text. Boldface terms in this Lab Manual can be found in the electronic glossary in the Utilities Folder. Clicking on the bold text in your *MacLaboratory* stack automatically accesses the correct *MacLaboratory* glossary entry.

Decision Time

Let's run our Decision Time experiment. Choose Run under the Experiment menu. The experiment has now started and the screen instructions are in effect; in other words, press the Z key to go on. If you dutifully do all the trials, when the experiment ends, the data window appears and you can view your data. You can't run the experiment again until you Save and/or Clear Data. Save your results as a Data file. You can open them later with a spreadsheet or statistical program. To use the Excel Macro, launch it and it will prompt you to load your saved data file and then automatically generate a report.

Excel™ Data Templates

A brief description of the functionality of the software can be found by choosing Help under the Apple menu. Take a moment to look through some of these topics.

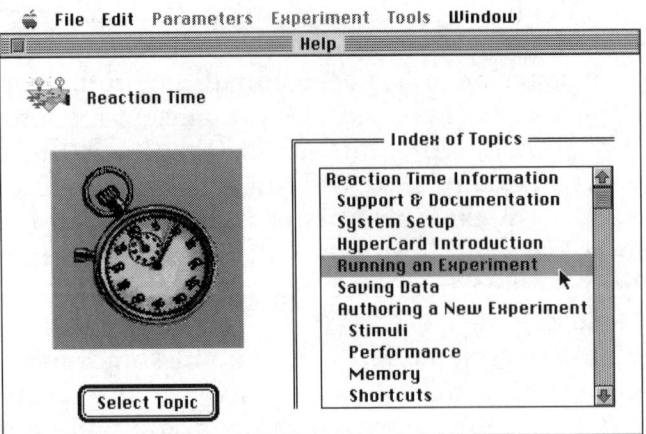

Read Me

In general, whenever you explore new software, you should examine the various Read Me files and other release notes that may be more recent than those contained in documentation.

If you have followed along with this Quick Start section so far, you should know how to navigate around *MacLaboratory* stacks. In addition, you should know how to run an existing Experiment file, what representative data look like, and how to find on-line help.

BASIC PURPOSE: LABORATORY MANUAL

No matter what your major, *MacLaboratory for Psychology* has a special purpose in science education beyond teaching you about psychology. Consider for a moment other laboratory courses you may have taken in high school or college. In all probability, they consisted of your following a "recipe," and your objective was to "get the right answer." If you were like most of us, half the time your test tube turned green instead of blue. You may even have thought it was OK to "fudge" your results to make things come out as the "right answer." Is that a good way to train students in scientific inquiry? In this course there aren't any "right answers" other than what your own data and analysis reveal. This may seem unusual to you at first, but the purpose is to show you how real research should be conducted. Say you are a business major. On your first job your boss might say, "I wonder if our product would sell better if we changed the color of our package." Your boss is proposing an experiment for which there may not be a "recipe." No doubt various people at work will have opinions about which color is the right answer. You can be the star, however, because you will know how to get the "facts" that will lead to the right answer! This course is designed to help you learn the basic skills to do any kind of research.

At the beginning of this course you will collect data and investigate problems in designing and analyzing experiments. By the end of the course, you will have planned and conducted your own Individual Research Project, where you can study something that may never have been looked at before. As one student put it, "In physics, we always dropped the same two cannonballs that everyone has dropped for three hundred years since Galileo, but in psychology, we designed real research experiments that had never been done before."

MacLaboratory for Psychology emphasizes the fundamentals of research in behavioral science. The main purpose of this Manual is to help you understand the proper application of the experimental method to behavioral problems. The popular (and sometimes professional) literature is replete with faulty experimentation and erroneous conclusions. One of our objectives is to provide you with the tools you'll need to critically analyze and evaluate the materials you read.

Laboratory work is essential in supplementing your classroom and textbook material to make it more vivid, give you practical experience with the kinds of things behavioral scientists do, and allow you to participate in handling the problems and techniques of the scientific method. From these laboratory exercises, you can see how knowledge about human nature is acquired through research. We believe in the truth of the adage that to hear is to forget, to see is to remember, to do is to understand. This Lab Manual is designed to help you with the "doing."

Since this may be your first introduction to the scientific study of behavior, we wish you good luck and express the hope that you will enjoy it as much as do those of us who have selected it as our life's work. Whether you have chosen this course as a start on a psychology major, as an elective, or perhaps to satisfy a requirement, you are likely to find much of interest in the study of human nature.

Douglas L. Chute
Robert S. Daniel
1994

INTRODUCTION

SECTION 1
EXPERIMENTAL METHODS

Fundamental to any science is the necessity for measurement. Psychology, in particular, faces a challenging problem in accurately qualifying and quantifying events. It is nearly impossible to be 100% certain about the occurrence of any event. Accordingly, the measurement of behavior deals in large part with probabilities, as is the case in all of science.

Another difficulty arises when the psychologist wishes to measure some general or loosely defined concept. For example, how can we "measure the mind"? A simple intelligence test is not satisfactory, for we cannot evaluate awareness, motivation, or other factors that might be considered part of the mind. Consequently, before measurement can begin, terms and concepts must be rigorously defined.

DEFINITIONS

Psychology generally copes with the problem of definition in two ways. The **behaviorist approach** quantifies and measures only those activities that can be observed. If a psychologist were interested in unhappiness in children, then the approach might be to measure the amount of time they cried. Here the overt crying behavior might be used to define the more general concept of "unhappiness." To relate behavior to a general concept is sometimes ill-advised, however. A child may have tears rolling down the cheeks from happiness. (Tickling can also do the trick.) To make assumptions about general concepts, the psychologist often relies on the **experimental method**. With this method, the experimenter manipulates one or more variables and controls as many other factors as possible. A pretty good guess can then be made about crying, whether it is the result of happiness or unhappiness.

A second way of coping with the problem of definition is to use an **operational definition**. There are some phenomena that we believe exist but that don't manifest themselves in an easily observed behavior—for example, "distractibility." The operational definition permits us to use a concept by defining it in terms of the experimental procedure. In the case of "distractibility," your instructor will set up a situation in the Motor Learning experiment where a presumably distracting situation will occur while the subject is engaged in the motor skills task of "mirror tracing." Distractibility is defined, then, by the operation of the particular experiment and its unique set of distracters. Does such a definition generalize to other distracters, such as to TV, roommates, or stereos during studying? An operational definition for a concept can be different from one experiment to the next; it depends solely on the procedure in the particular experiment in question.

Definitions are important because they aid communication and are the basic building blocks of any science. Most problems you will face in this course can be solved by having a thorough understanding of the terms and concepts introduced in each project.

THE EXPERIMENTAL METHOD

Psychology uses a systematic way of collecting data called the **experimental method**. In an experiment, the investigator observes one event after having manipulated another. At the same time, other events, which might influence the one being studied, are controlled. Causality can be determined if it follows that the observed event changes in some kind of orderly fashion with the manipulation.

In psychology experiments, the observed events are behavioral events in human or animal subjects. The manipulated events may be stimulus features, physiological features, social features, or other psychological features. For example, an industrial psychologist might manipulate the color of lighting in a room and observe the behavior of people working in that room. We would call the color variations the **independent variable** and the observed change in behavior the **dependent variable**, because the color is the antecedent and the behavior the consequent. To some degree the behavior may be said to depend on the color. Do you know which colors are best in a work environment or do you just have an opinion?

If we are to be convinced of the effect of color, it is most important that we be sure that no other causal factors influence the observations. For example, if the experimenter used one color on cloudy days and another on bright days, we could not determine whether the observed effect was caused by room color or by the weather. Therefore, an experimenter must learn to control features in the situation other than the one he or she wants to manipulate. If that control is successful, and if we observe an orderly relationship between manipulated and observed events, then we are in a good position to draw inferences about how behavior is modified or, in a sense, caused. This example of color, by the way, comes from an area of psychology in **human factors** or industrial research. In fact, the color, lighting, and atmosphere of a workplace affect many different behaviors, as does change itself. Change seems to improve attitudes and productivity paradoxically, even if it appears to be a change for the worse. A problem for the researcher, then, is the possibility that an experiment itself intrudes in the normal state of affairs. Perhaps you can think of similar phenomena, such as the color and packaging of consumer products and the advertising claims of improvement and change that accompany many of them.

The main purpose of this part of the course is to illustrate some basic techniques by which scientists control and manipulate variables so that a cause-and-effect relationship can be established and a measure of certainty or probability concerning the results may be obtained. The most important thing you should get out of this section of your Lab Manual is the logic by which causality can be established by the experimental method.

Psychology gains information about behavior in many ways. In general, the **scientific method** includes not only the experimental method but also other activities, such as accurate observation in natural settings, detailed descriptions, and classification schemes.

STATISTICS

We are bombarded with statistical information, not only in scientific reports but also in the popular media. Many people hold the view that "there are lies, there are damn lies, and there are statistics." Can you prove anything with statistics? What are the proper uses and applications of statistics?

There are two basic classes of statistics: **descriptive statistics**, which summarizes large sets of data; and **inferential statistics**, which test the probability that two or more sets of data are in all likelihood different from one another. Descriptive statistics include those that measure the **central tendency** of a set or distribution of numbers. For example, the **mean**, or average, is used to summarize the central tendency, or middle, of a grade distribution on a class examination. The **median**, as a measure of central tendency, is often used when the mean might in fact misrepresent the "center" of an actual distribution. For example, suppose that in a small class one person gets 100% and everyone else fails. The mean might work out to imply that the class average is passing; the median would show a failing record. Aside from certain mathematical rules, there is obviously a matter of judgment regarding the appropriate ways to use statistics. By the way, the same issue of judgment applies to graphic descriptions of data. If a graph "crunches up" or "spreads out," the vertical scale differences might appear to be minimized or blown out of proportion, respectively.

As a consumer of research, you need to be sensitive to the appropriate use of statistics in the description of data and in making inferences about the significance of any observed differences among sets of data. Always evaluate the judgment calls the author has made, and determine for yourself whether the statistical information is appropriate to support the conclusions being made. You are the best "lie detector" vis-à-vis statistics.

If the experimental design is flawed or if there are uncontrolled variables in an experiment, it is impossible to make a definitive cause-and-effect statement based on what was done with statistics, or computers for that matter. Sometimes subjects are tempted to cheat in psychological experiments, or as a matter of perversity, they sometimes try and mess things up. Thus, the act of conducting an experiment itself disturbs the situation, a sort of psychological Heisenberg principle. In Project 1, on extrasensory perception, people are usually very motivated to do well. After you have completed that project, think about the types of controls that would be needed to ensure that intentional or unintentional factors were not involved.

PROJECT 1

MEASURING EXTRASENSORY PERCEPTION

A few years ago I had the pleasure of serving on a faculty with psychologists David Marks and Dick Kammann. One of their specialties was demonstrating the tricks used by various charlatans and sociopaths to convince unsuspecting people that they had extrasensory powers. They demonstrated how to bend keys, spoons and solid steel bars by the supposed application of mind over matter, referred to as **psychokinesis**. They could make watches that had not run for years tick away again. They even showed how scientists can be deceived by clever magicians. For example, some of you may have seen **telepathy** demonstrations, where a person on stage appears to be able to read the mind of someone who sealed the contents of an envelope. Are they reading minds? About half the adult population believes that this is possible. Yet no demonstration of these or other reputed phenomena, such as **clairvoyance** or **precognition**, has stood up to scientific scrutiny. Since these are tricks, it is often best to have a magician consultant like James Randi (the Amazing Randi), who specializes in exposing the tricks used by these magicians.

In this project we conduct an experiment where trickery (by us or by you, the subject) is not likely to be employed, where sensory cues or clues are probably absent, and where biases on the part of the computer, subjects, or the experimenter are not likely to have a large effect. It actually would not be difficult to cheat in this experiment, but then you would know that you didn't have ESP. In fact, subjects in psychology experiments tend to either try and help the experimenters or mess them up. This is why some psychologists have used deception in their experiments. The experiments in this manual do not use deception, in part because deception raises ethical issues that make **informed consent** and **voluntary withdrawal** more difficult to ensure.

In our ESP experiment we present one of five stimuli—a circle, wave, square, cross, or star—and you have to guess which is coming up next in a random presentation.

If you do significantly better than chance (20% correct), then we have to come up with an explanation for this observed result. If you believe you might have ESP, or *psi* powers, you can use any psychic strategy you wish to try and influence the presentation of stimuli and therefore your probability of making accurate predictions. For example, in precognition, one supposedly has the ability to foretell events—in this case, which object comes up next. If you wish, try and use precognition when you run the experiment. Alternatively, because of the way the experiment is constructed in the software, you may want to try clairvoyance as a strategy. The actual stimulus is hidden by the computer and appears only at the end of the guessing period. A third psychic strategy that you might want to try is psychokinesis, where you theoretically compel the computer to show the stimulus that matches your guess.

1. Purposes

To measure the success rate at guessing a future event compared to its actual probability. To generate an individual performance record and a class performance record. To illustrate measures of central tendency and principles of graphic representation.

2. Apparatus

Macintosh microcomputer and the experiment file ESP Experiment with the application Reaction Time. Graphing may be done by hand or with a spreadsheet like Excel, as your instructor requires.

Measuring Extrasensory Perception

3. Procedure

Each student will launch the Experiment file. When you are ready, choose Run under the Experiment menu and follow the instructions. Type an entry for your guess about which symbol will appear. You must type the *exact* name of the stimulus. There is a time limit, so you must finish your entry by the time you hear the beep. Then you will see what the stimulus actually was. When the experiment is finished, halt its running and save an electronic copy on your disk. If you plan on using the Excel Macro for data analysis, you must use the Save As... command and name and save a Data Only file.

4. Data Analysis

A total of 25 experimental trials will be run. The stimuli are randomized, with the constraint that there are five presentations each of the circle, wave, square, cross, and star. For this experiment, "part right" will not count nor will we be using the Reaction Time data.

You can use the Excel Macro to automatically calculate your "hit rate" as a percent correct and then plot your results. However, we recommend you hand score your data in Table 1-1 (on p. 27) so you are clear about some of the basic procedures in statistical description.

```
                    ESP Sample ◆ Data
Page range: 1 to 8                              Started
                                           Sep 25, 1995
                                             4:31:30 PM
Experiment run with 256 colors/grays.
                                              Completed
                                           Sep 25, 1995
                                             4:54:00 PM
```

Trial	Page	Correct Response Input	Time (ms)	Incorrect Response Input	Time (ms)
3	3	square	2954		0
4	5		0	star	1343
5	7		0	square	3698
6	4	wave	979		0
7	6		0	cross	2549
8	6	star	1282		0
9	7	cross	1843		0
10	5	circle	2284		0
11	4		0	square	1812

If you look at the sample data illustrated here, you will see that each of the "experiment pages" from 3 to 7 has a single correct answer. The pages are repeated in random order for the full 25 trials. Thus, when page 3 appears in the data, you know that the correct response should have been "square"; page 4 is "wave"; page 5, "circle"; page 6, "star"; and page 7, "cross." In Table 1-1, tabulate the frequency of correct responses for each of the stimuli.

A table of raw data often seems too complex and unorganized to enable us to draw any conclusions about the ability of the class as a whole to accurately predict the appearance of a stimulus. It would be more convenient to have a summary, or description, that would indicate the central value for the cluster of numbers in the **distribution** of guesses. The **central tendency** for the distribution is such a summary. The three most common **descriptive statistics** that summarize central tendency are the **mean**, the **mode**, and the **median**. The mean is the arithmetic average and can be represented by the following formula:

The Arithmetic Mean

$$\overline{X} = \frac{\Sigma x_i}{N}$$

Σ = (sigma) sum up

x_i = each score

N = the number of numbers

Most of you are familiar with the average, or mean. The mode is less familiar but simply means the most common score. If you look at the body of raw data in Table 1-1, you will see that subjects will have gotten various scores, from zero to as many as five correct. The mode is the most common, or frequent, score and is most often used when data are **nominal** in nature. For example, it makes no sense to ask "What is the average fruit in the produce section of a market?" It would make sense to ask "Which is the most common, or modal, way, if you will, of comparing apples to oranges?"

The median is simply the midmost number when a distribution is arranged in an ordered series. For example, if you have three observations *arranged in order of size*, the median is the middle one. If you have four observations, the median is the score halfway between the second and third observations. Expanding this simple example into a principle, you can see that if you have an uneven number of observations, you count the number of observations, divide by 2, and add ½ to the result. Count observations from either end of the ordered series, and when you come to the observation in that numerical position, that is your median. If you have an even number of observations, divide by 2, find that case, and then determine half the distance (difference) between it and the next one in order. Practice this procedure on the following examples, which have been properly arranged:

The Median (50th Percentile)
Calculate the median for the ordered series below:
Median
5, 7, 9, 11, 13   _____
22, 31, 37, 42, 51, 55, 60, 69, 75   _____
103, 103, 105, 106, 107, 107, 124, 152, 175   _____

In general, the median is the score that has an equal number of scores above and below it.

In addition to central tendency, it is often desirable to have a summary descriptive statistic to measure how stretched out or bunched together the numbers are in a distribution. One such measure of **variability** is the **range**. In its simplest form, the range of a distribution is the difference between the highest and the lowest numbers. Suppose the lowest percent correct in our ESP experiment was 10 and the highest 50, then the range would be 50 – 10 = 40.

5. DISPLAYING THE RESULTS

Scientists typically show their results in the form of a graph, which provides a more vivid representation than you can get from a table or other form. It is an example of the old adage that a picture is worth a thousand words. A graph consists of a pair of axes, one representing the **independent variable** and the other representing the **dependent variable**. The axes are arranged perpendicular to each other so that data plotted in the graph illustrate the functional relationship between the two variables. By convention, the independent variable is represented on the horizontal axis (sometimes called the *x*-axis, or abscissa) and the dependent variable is represented on the vertical axis (sometimes called the *y*-axis, or ordinate). For this first project there are different graphs you might make, depending on what you would like to illustrate or what your instructor might require. Whether you are constructing your graph by hand or using software, you need to follow some general principles that normally apply to all graphs used for scientific communication: Graphs have a title, a legend or key, and labeled axes that indicate units, and they should not be designed to visually mislead a casual observer concerning the magnitude of an effect.

Suppose you want to plot a bar graph showing your individual performance compared with the class averages for each of the target stimuli. If you use a spreadsheet like Excel, you enter the relevant data into a Worksheet, select your data, and then choose to make a New Chart from it, as illustrated:

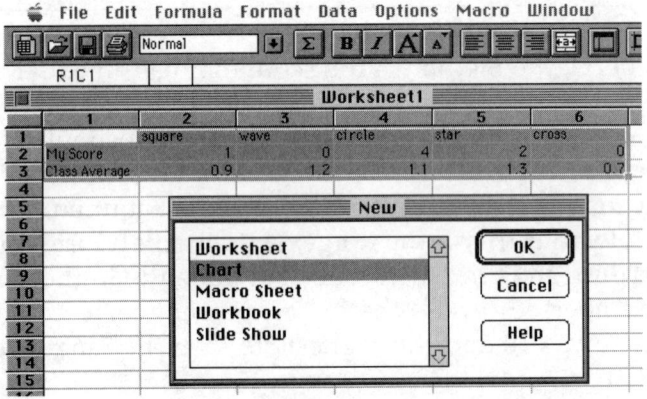

Using the appropriate commands in the software, you Attach Text to the *x*-axis and the *y*-axis and make a descriptive title. You also Add a Legend. The result should look something like the following, whether you are using software or graphing by hand.

Measuring Extrasensory Perception

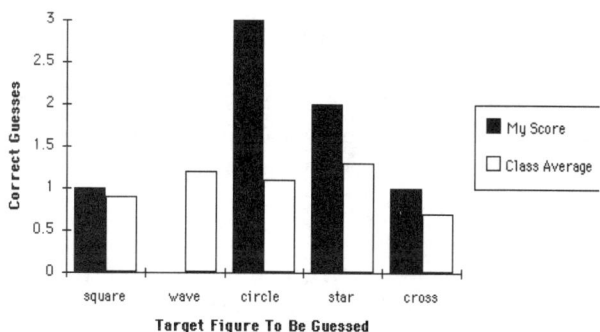

Another type of graph that might be useful to illustrate the distribution of our class data is a frequency polygon. On the abscissa are the various possible scores from 0 to 5 correct hits taken from the class raw data. The ordinate indicates the frequency of scores in each category. Notice how the distribution looks quite similar to the **normal curve**. Using all the scores from your class data, construct a frequency polygon to show your results. Your Excel spreadsheet or some other graphics application should be used to produce a quality finished product that resembles the illustration below. In this case a three-dimensional view has been used. Be careful that your artful presentations of a graph do not obscure its meaning.

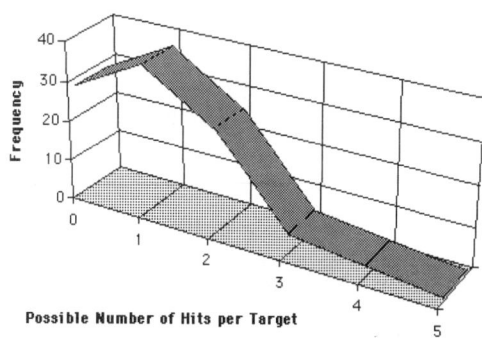

6. INTERPRETATION

The following questions are for discussion, study, and review.

A. Define each of the following terms: normal curve, range, mean, median, mode, frequency polygon, functional relationship, abscissa, ordinate, raw data, nominal data, informed consent, voluntary withdrawal.

B. You have now completed your first experiment in this course. What is an experiment? How does it differ from other ways of gaining understanding? Contrast a scientist's definition of science with the dictionary definition. Why do you suppose they are so different?

C. Do you think our experiment gave people a fair chance to demonstrate ESP powers? Do you think our results are valid?

D. What factors were not controlled in this experiment? How could the experiment be improved?

E. Can you think of two or three hypotheses that deal with ESP that might form the basis for your Individual Research Project?

Measuring Extrasensory Perception 25

Student _____ Section _____ Due Date _____

MEASURING EXTRASENSORY PERCEPTION

1. What is the modal value for the number of correct guesses in the class data?

   What is the median value for the percent correct in the class data?

   What is the range of percent correct in the class data?

2. What was your personal overall percent correct?

   Write a hypothesis about why you think you achieved that result.

3. What factors were not controlled in this experiment? How could the experiment be improved?

4. Write an **abstract** explaining what was done in this project and what your conclusions are, based on the class results. See the notes concerning abstracts in the IRP section at the back of this manual.

5. Include any additional material your instructor may require.

6. Attach Table 1-1 and your graph.

TABLE 1-1
ESP Experiment Class Data Summary

Sub-ject No.	square page 3	wave page 4	circle page 5	star page 6	cross page 7	Total Correct	Average Correct per page	% Correct
1.								
2.								
3.								
4.								
5.								
6.								
7.								
8.								
9.								
10.								
11.								
12.								
13.								
14.								
15.								
16.								
17.								
18.								
19.								
20.								
$\overline{X} =$								

PROJECT 2

MEASURING MOTOR LEARNING

In many life situations, we are faced with acquiring new skills that require muscular coordination, perceptual input, and feedback. Fortunately, we can usually draw on a rich repertoire of previous experiences. Different people, however, have had different experiences. For some, their environment has provided an advantage, and they find themselves more talented than others at acquiring new skills. For others, nature, that is, their genetic make-up, provides the advantage, and they seem inherently talented—for example, "natural" athletes. In order to assess such talent, psychologists have devised a fairly simple group of tasks, such as mirror tracing, for which most people have had little specific practice. The mirror-tracing task allows the psychologist to assess one of the seven basic motor skills: eye–hand coordination. By tracing a simple outline viewed through a computer "mirror," left and right are reversed. (For the Macintosh, "mouse" movements are reversed for the same effect as the mirror.) A person with talent in learning new eye–hand coordination will acquire the task more quickly than others. By the way, if you happen not to do well at this task, take heart. The seven different types of motor skills are not very closely related. Thus, if someone is poor at one of them, like eye–hand coordination, they may well be good at another, like reaction time or routine movement. In other words, a total "klutz" is very rare, as is the "all-round athlete."

Psychologists have used some interesting applications of motor skills learning in the "real" world. For example, in **sports psychology** such tests have been used to identify people with exceptional athletic ability even though they may have had little experience with a particular sport. Once identified, they are coached in that particular sport. Baseball and football in North America and Olympic sports in Eastern European countries have benefited from this approach.

Neuropsychology uses motor skills tests and training techniques to assess and rehabilitate patients suffering from neurological disorders. In fact, these tasks are most often used in such clinical situations.

As a demonstration of interest to students, we use the mirror-tracing tasks to collect data so that you may plot your own individual learning curves for eye–hand coordination. You can compare this to normative, or average, results of other North Americans in your age group. A second demonstration is designed to illustrate the effects of distraction on the acquisition of new learning. While doing the mirror-tracing task, you are faced with a series of distractions, such as roommates, radio, or television to see how these might affect your studying.

In a third demonstration, we use the pursuit rotor function (where the target moves) to illustrate the effects of massed versus distributed practice—that is, to find the best temporal arrangement of training schedules to optimize performance. In massed practice, all learning is concentrated at one time. In distributed practice, learning trials are spaced out with rest intervals in between. This demonstration might be thought of as a model to illustrate the effects on learning of cramming (massed practice) versus spread-out studying (distributed practice). Both, by the way, seem better than not studying at all.

Measuring Motor Learning

You might wish to develop your own experiments for your Individual Research Project requirements, ones you can conduct using the software applications. For example, women often do better than men at some motor skills tasks. Is this true for mirror tracing and pursuit rotor? How would you design an experiment to test this hypothesis? How would you analyze your data? As another example, people with excessive muscle bulk, like those who "pump" too much "iron," often do poorly on such tasks. How could this hypothesis be tested? You might also consider another important variable in motor skills learning, namely feedback. What effect does the knowledge, or lack of it, have on the trial-to-trial measures of performance? Generally, such feedback results in faster learning. Before you begin work on your own experiments, discuss your plans with your laboratory instructor.

1. Purposes

To determine if distraction is disruptive of performance. To generate an individual acquisition curve and compare it to normative data. To learn fundamental concepts of experimental control of random error and progressive error. To summarize with descriptive statistics.

2. Apparatus

Macintosh microcomputer and the experiment files for Mirror Tracing with the application Motor Skills.

Motor Skills

3. Procedure

The instructor will conduct the project as a demonstration experiment, where students will be grouped in pairs, one person serving as experimenter and the other as subject.

3.1 The Task

Performance is automatically recorded by the computer. The subject attempts to use the mouse to trace along a 5-mm-wide path in the form of a 5-pointed star. The subject avoids touching the sides of the path, because when the cursor goes off the track the software records error-time. The objective is to trace as far as possible in each trial while touching the sides as little as possible.

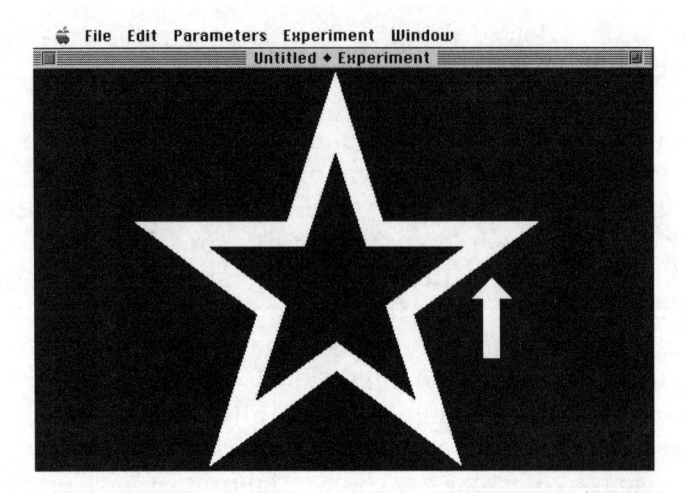

Prior to computerization, the task was made difficult by requiring subjects to observe their performance via a mirror. Because few people had practice in this task, it yielded a measure of the subject's ability to learn new motor skills. With the Macintosh, the movements of the "mouse" are reversed for both up and down and left and right, making the performance similarly difficult and, again, yielding an opportunity to observe learning of a new motor behavior.

3.2 Scoring

Performance may be scored in several ways, but we use a combination score which recognizes that the longer the path traced, the better, and the smaller the error time, the better. Hence, the score is the distance in centimeters divided by the error time in seconds, and the larger the score, the better the performance. Such a combined score can have its problems. For example, if no errors are made, an awkward situation of dividing by zero occurs. The computer arbitrarily divides by 1 for any error score of less than 1. Distance traveled and time off target are also recorded by the program.

3.3 Feedback

Feedback to the subject has an important effect on learning for any type of task. For this demonstration, all subjects in all conditions hear a tone when they go off target, which keeps the effects

Measuring Motor Learning

of this factor constant across conditions, making it a **controlled variable**.

3.4 Experimental Design

Our strategy in doing this experiment is to produce a change in the situation (distraction vs. no distraction) in order to determine if it will modify the subject's behavior. In experimental terms, this is the manipulation of the **independent variable**. We purposefully insert or remove the distracter. In order to make a cause-and-effect statement about the effects of distraction on performance, we need to hold all other variables constant, allowing only one, the independent variable, to change. Thus, if the behavioral performance, the **dependent variable**, also changes, then we can infer that the independent variable caused the observed change. We might hypothesize that in this case, distraction lowers performance scores.

Because two general types of error—progressive error and random error—are controlled in this experiment, a cause-and-effect relationship can be inferred.

3.5 Progressive Error

In our experiment, we want to investigate the effect of distraction on performance. Of necessity, we must collect data with distraction present at one time and with distraction absent at a different time. Will the condition we choose to do first have an effect on the one we do second? If we find a difference, will it be *caused* by the presence or absence of distraction? Perhaps such a difference was simply the result of distraction preceding no-distraction (or vice versa)?

In more general terms, what we want to find out first is this: Will prior performance influence future performance? If it does, then we are obligated to find some way to remove or nullify the effect. In experimental terms, we are faced with the possibility of **progressive error** being an **uncontrolled variable**, which must be handled so that it is instead changed into a **controlled variable**.

In our experiment, progressive error is most likely to come from learning. That is, the subject is going to improve with practice. Thus, if we had no distraction first, followed by distraction second, we might see that the latter was superior because of the progressive effect of practice and not because distraction actually improves performance. Other factors, aside from learning, occur over time in experiments and are, therefore, potential sources of progressive error. These include boredom, fatigue, hunger, and sleepiness—anything that changes over time.

3.6 Random Error

Another kind of error that is always present in behavioral research is **random error**. This term refers to the small differences that occur from time to time no matter how hard you try to repeat everything exactly. For example, you have probably never written your signature twice in precisely the same way. Variability from random error is commonly controlled by averaging. Behavioral scientists generally take a number of trials or observations, then use the mean to represent them. This procedure results in an estimate of the "true score," and it assumes that random error (sometimes increasing, sometimes decreasing the observed score) cancels out, or at least tends to do so. Normative data represent the average or mean performance of a large number of subjects. Compared to the individual learning curve you will be making of your own performance, such data show less of the random variability that occurs in an individual from trial to trial.

Summaries, whether statistics or graphs, can be misleading or difficult to interpret. For example, the average family has 2¼ children. What is a ¼ child? If you compare the group learning curve with your own individual curve, the two may be quite different. In fact, some psychologists might argue that the **incremental learning** apparent in a group curve is a total misrepresentation and that learning occurs in an **all-or-none** fashion. For any summarizing procedure, care must be taken to ensure that the summary accurately represents the underlying data.

Remember that a subject will change somewhat regardless, so we have to look for a change in performance that is greater, or more impressive, than any random changes if we are to be convinced that our manipulation of an independent variable has had an influence.

Measuring Motor Learning

3.7 Sequencing the Independent Variable Through Counterbalancing

The experimenter will give the subject a total of six trials under conditions of quiet and another six trials under conditions of distraction. The experimenter will also determine the nature and extent of the distracting stimuli. We manage or control for progressive change by taking three trials under quiet, three trials under distraction, three more trials under distraction, and, finally, three trials under quiet. Thus, we are using the **experimental design** known as the ABBA **counterbalancing** sequence. In this scheme, the influence of level A of the independent variable (here "quiet") is applied at each end of the progressive sequence and level B (distraction) is applied to the two middle segments. The theory is that the average influence of progressive change at the two end segments should approximate the average influence in the two middle segments, canceling the effect of progressive change when the two A segments are combined and the two B segments are combined. The procedure should allow the differential A–B treatment manipulation (i.e., the independent variable) to "show through" the otherwise confusing influence of progressive change. (You will need to master the logic of counterbalancing if you are to use this in the future.) When managed in this fashion, progressive error is said to be a *controlled variable*. Notice that in this case progressive error is not really eliminated, but it is arranged to influence the A and B levels of the independent variable approximately equally.

Of course, many other methods are available for controlling unwanted variables. Compare counterbalancing to the **Latin square**. In counterbalancing we have a **within-subjects design**, where the same subject provides all the scores. The Latin square creates two groups. One receives the conditions in the AB order, the other in the BA order. The Latin square requires more than one group, which could be a source of confounding if the groups are not identical.

4. Data Analysis

A total of 12 trials will be run. The conditions of quiet and distraction are organized by trial in counterbalanced order, as indicated in Table 2-1. Find the mean for each of the two conditions.

Although the mean of quiet and distracted trials provides a good description of the central tendency, it would be advantageous to have some summary descriptive statistic to indicate the variability in our data. Variability can be thought of as an indication of how different each score is from the mean, or center, of a group of scores. As such, it is often expressed as the average amount (sum of all the differences divided by the number) that each score is from the mean. To solve a little mathematical problem with the plus and minus signs canceling each other out, these different scores are initially squared. The **standard deviation** reverses the process, as it were, and is the square root of the variance. A conceptual formula is the following:

The Standard Deviation

$$SD = \sqrt{\frac{\Sigma(x_i - \bar{X})^2}{N}}$$

Σ = (sigma) sum up

$x_i - \bar{X}$ = each score − the mean

N = the number of numbers

You should recognize the similarity of the formula to the mean. One important use of the standard deviation is to permit the comparison of any individual's score to a large distribution, or **population**, of scores, as we will see in the next project.

5. Interpretation

The following questions are for discussion, study, and review.

A. Define each of the terms introduced: progressive error, random error, unwanted variable, controlled variable, principle of the single variable, standard deviation, experimental design, counterbalanced order, experimental and control conditions. Carefully distinguish between a controlled variable and the independent variable.

B. How would you arrange a counterbalanced design if you had three conditions, A, B, and C, instead of two? What kind of functional relationship between the unwanted variable and

Measuring Motor Learning

the dependent variable is assumed in counterbalancing? Can the assumption be tested? Should it be tested?

C. The factor causing unwanted progressive change in the present project was undoubtedly learning. What other factor might be expected to cause progressive change? The task for this project was deliberately chosen to show a strong progressive change, but of course in most research it is more subtle. Nevertheless, it is always potentially troublesome. What other experimental design might be used to control for progressive error? Can you think of a reason why some other method might have been more appropriate?

D. What practical application might be made from the results of this study? What determines the degree to which outside stimuli are distracting? Have you had experiences studying with the radio or TV that might supply a reasonable hypothesis? Can you design a study to test the disturbing effects of some stimulus in a real-life situation?

E. Does the difference between the "quiet" mean and the "distraction" mean in Table 2-1 appear to be a large enough difference (in relation to normal random variability) to convince you that distraction does change performance? The next project allows us to determine the significance of an observed difference.

F. Relate the early difficulties of the subject in mirror tracing to the disparity in "cue feedback" from the eyes and from the hand.

G. Why was "knowledge-of-results feedback" controlled?

H. Can random error or progressive error ever be eliminated?

Student _____ Section _____ Due Date _____

MEASURING MOTOR LEARNING

1. Briefly define in your own words the following terms:

Counterbalancing

Standard Deviation

Neuropsychology

Random Error

Independent Variable

Within-subjects design

2. Write a Methods section detailing the subjects, apparatus, and procedures used. Refer to the IRP at the back of the manual for specific guidelines on writing a Methods section for a report.

3. Using the same procedures as in the project, arrange a meeting with your laboratory partner so that you can collect data, with your roles of experimenter and subject reversed. Run six quiet and six distracted trials. Use your imagination regarding distracters (e.g., TV, boyfriend/girlfriend). You can both then plot a graph of individual performance by trials. Using Table 2-2, complete the means and standard deviations from your own data on each condition. Collect data carefully, and preserve them for Project 3.

4. Include any additional material your instructor may require.

5. Attach Tables 2-1 and 2-2 and your graph.

Measuring Motor Learning

TABLE 2-1
MIRROR-TRACING PERFORMANCE

\multicolumn{4}{c}{Independent Variable}			
\multicolumn{2}{c}{Quiet}	\multicolumn{2}{c}{Distracted}	
Trial	Score	Trial	Score
1.		4.	
2.		5.	
3.		6.	
10.		7.	
11.		8.	
12.		9.	
$\overline{X} =$		$\overline{X} =$	
Difference Between the Means			

Your Subject's Name	
Experimenter's Name	

TABLE 2-2

PERSONAL PERFORMANCE ON MIRROR-TRACING

Independent Variable					$SD = \sqrt{\dfrac{\Sigma(x_i - \overline{X})^2}{N}}$			
Quiet				Distracted				
Trial	Score	$x_i - \overline{X}$	$(x_i - X)^2$	Trial	Score	$x_i - \overline{X}$	$(x_i - X)^2$
1.				4.			
2.				5.			
3.				6.			
10.				7.			
11.				8.			
12.				9.			
Σ		Σ		Σ		Σ	
$\overline{X} =$		/N		$\overline{X} =$		/N	
		$\sqrt{}$				$\sqrt{}$	

PROJECT 3

PRINCIPLES OF STATISTICAL INFERENCE

Statistics are used in many aspects of modern life, not just in research experiments. We run across statistics in business, engineering, and everyday newspaper reports. Probably most of us also have had an ingrained suspicion that statistics can be used to "prove just about anything." Although this is actually not completely true, you would be wise to know quite a bit about statistics because there is no doubt that a certain "spin" or another can disguise one reality or promote another.

Descriptive statistics, like the mean and the standard deviation, summarize data. Inferential statistics, like the **sign test** or the *t*-**test**, provide probability estimates regarding the relationship between one set of data and another. In this lab and generally throughout the course, we use a type of inferential statistic called **nonparametric statistics**. Typically, these are mathematically much simpler than parametric statistics since they are more concerned with the direction of differences in observations than with calculations of their magnitude. We use nonparametric statistics to permit you to focus more on concepts and less on calculations. Nonparametric statistics are less commonly used, however, if a choice is available, because they are less powerful.

The most important thing about statistics is that they allow us to make informed decisions. The human brain is a very poor estimator of probability. It can be easily overwhelmed by too much information or, in some cases, it can be easily distracted by salient and nonrepresentative events. Statistics are not intrinsically evil, but you should be cautious if they are at odds with common sense.

1. Purposes

To derive quantified descriptions of the effects of distraction on the motor learning task of mirror tracing as conducted in Project 2. To test the significance of any observed effects. To make standardized comparisons.

2. Procedure

Before we turn our attention to the details of this procedure, it is important that you be aware of two problems. First, the abbreviated data analysis and interpretation you did in Project 2 was done on one subject . For example, one person (or a few) may have shown that distraction had no effect or even the opposite effect from that predicted. However good a description of mirror-tracing behavior that may have been, it is not sufficient for making generalizations about people in general, or even about students who enroll in psychology. The first problem then is the issue of **sampling**, and generalization to a **population**.

Another problem relates to the experiment itself. A number of psychological factors can alter the results of an experiment you have conducted on yourself. With a little thought, you might discover some of these. Maybe you thought this was a trivial or

Principles of Statistical Inference

"Mickey Mouse" thing to do. Maybe you considered it an imposition to have to spend your own time actually doing it. Maybe you fooled around instead of considering how important it might be for each student to use a **standardized procedure** for collecting data. All of these are symptoms of a phenomenon that plagues science, sometimes called the **Rosenthal effect**, where the biases or desires of experimenters and subjects can alter the results. Even if you weren't consciously hoping for a particular outcome—say that quiet is superior to distraction—your own wishes might still have unconsciously (or worse, consciously,) affected the results. How should such problems be solved in experimental design? What is a blind or **double-blind** design ?

Data Analysis. In this project the instructor will use the group data from project 2 to explain and illustrate the step-by-step procedure in deriving estimates of significance. Then each student will use these techniques to analyze the group data to determine if distraction has a significant effect on performance.

To prepare for the demonstration by the instructor, be sure that your scores are entered in Table 3-1. When the instructor calls for these data, each student will orally report the two means, and you will need to copy all of these into your table in order to follow through with the instructor's demonstration.

3. PROBABILITY ANALYSIS OF DATA

You may see in Table 3-2 or in the graph from Project 2 that there is an observed difference between the two experimental conditions. However, we had no method for evaluating the magnitude and importance of the difference. We might ask what are the chances that such a difference could have occurred by chance alone. Fortunately, we have available the methods of **inferential statistics**, which provide a far more exact method for determining if an observed difference is convincing. In this case, we use the **sign test**. Many other such tests are available for different situations.

Looking at the problem in terms of our present data, you would probably agree that in order to be convincing, the differences between the two conditions must either be greater than the variability from trial to trial, or they must be consistently in the same direction from subject to subject. Of course, we might be convinced if we found some favorable combination of these two criteria. The sign test uses the second criterion. It is appropriate as a test of differences when scores can be paired, as in our present data; that is, there is a score for the quiet performance and one for the distracted performance that "belong together" because they came from the same person in our **within-subjects** experimental design. By the use of the sign test, and its table of interpretation, we can determine if enough of our subjects do better for the quiet condition to convince us that we have a difference that is a function of the manipulation of the independent variable and not merely determined by random error. This procedure is called a **test of significance**, and it is accomplished by testing the **null hypothesis**. The idea of this test is quite straightforward; we guess (hypothesize) that there is no difference (null) and test to see if this is probably true or probably false. The rather cautious typical scientist looks for no more than a 1% probability that the null hypothesis is correct (99% probability that it is not). In some fields where there is more variability, a 5% probability (95% probability against) may be allowed. You may have seen a scientific journal article where the null hypothesis has been rejected and a probability value is given—for example p 0.01 or p 0.05, which means the same thing. In everyday language we would say that if a result has only a 1 in 100 chance of really being no different, then our experimental result is **significant** (at p 0.01, or 1%, level).

Step 1. Use the last column of Table 3-1 to record the signs. If a subject's quiet score is superior to (larger than) his or her distracted score, then put a plus sign in the column for that subject. If the opposite is the case, use a minus sign. If the scores are tied use a zero. Now count the number of + signs and enter this count at the bottom of the column.

Step 2. Count the total number of plus and minus signs in Table 3-1 (do not count zeros), then find this number in the first column of Table A, headed "Sample Size (N)." Look in the same row over in column 2, headed "5% level." If your count of **plus signs** at the bottom of the last column of Table 3-1 is equal to or larger than this figure, then the quiet condition is indeed superior.

Let us take a final look at the logic of this procedure. If there really is no difference between doing mirror tracing while quiet and doing it while distracted, we would expect about half the subjects to do better in one, and half in the other condition. For this type of task, random variability would make it unlikely we would have very many "perfect" ties or zeros. To be sure a difference is not due to chance (a term we use to refer to all uncontrolled factors collectively), we look for many more than half the cases to show up in the predicted direction. Table 3A has been worked out by statisticians to show what proportion is required for the degree of confidence (convincibility or probability) we are looking for. Those of you who will later take a course in statistics will learn more sophisticated methods for a greater variety of situations but the basic logic is still the same.

It might help to think of the sign test in terms of coin tosses or roulette wheels (red or black). If you were playing such a game of chance, you would want to make sure that the coin or wheel was unbiased and fair (unless maybe it was your coin or wheel, but that would be unethical). That is, you expect the **null hypothesis** to be true; namely, the game is not "fixed." So, for example, if a coin is tossed 15 times and comes up heads (or tails) 6, 7, 8, or 9 times, you have no statistical reason to believe the coin is fixed. If 11 heads or tails show up, you conclude there is a real probability the coin is biased since the chance of this occurring is only 5% (Table 3A). For an unbiased coin, the chances of any toss are 50% or 0.50. Two tosses in a row the same would be 0.50 x 0.50 or 0.25 and so on.

4. Assessment of Individual Scores

4.1

This project illustrates an important concept that helps psychologists interpret an individual's performance on such standardized tests as IQ measures. Many types of IQ tests contain subsets that deal with motor performance using tasks like mirror tracing. So far, you have learned how to derive a measure of central tendency (especially the mean) and a measure of variability (especially the standard deviation). You learned also that these two measures can be used to summarize, or represent, a larger body of observations (the distribution). Now we learn still another useful application of these two statistics that will give us an even better representation of an individual score or observation.

TABLE 3A

SIGN TEST OF STATISTICAL SIGNIFICANCE

Sample Size (N) Subtract 1 from N for each tie	Number of plus signs required when the direction of difference is predicted (One-tailed test)	
	5% Level	1% Level
5	5	5
6	6	6
7	7	7
8	8	8
9	9	9
10	10	10
11	11	11
12	12	12
13	13	13
14	14	14
15	15	15
16	16	16
17	17	17
18	18	18
19	19	19
20	20	20
21	21	21
22	22	22
23	23	23
24	24	24
25	25	25

Principles of Statistical Inference

4.2

In most instances of behavioral research, it is not practical to measure an entire **population** of subjects. Generally, a **representative sample** of the population is chosen for the study. If the sample is well selected, then it can be used to "stand for" the population, and a generalization to the whole population can be defended. This is the logic supporting the methods used in public opinion polling, such as the Gallup Poll.

4.3

We make similar types of projections in behavioral research. Instead of predicting the outcome of a vote, we predict the value of the central tendency and of the variability (the **parameters**) of the population distribution. If our normative sample is truly representative, then the parameters of the sample distribution can be used to give a close approximation of the parameters of the population. For our purposes, we shall accept the mean and standard deviation of the normative data as the best estimate of the population parameters.

4.4

Many natural phenomena are normally distributed: height and weight of adults, IQs, personality scores, number of letters in surnames, and many others.

Whenever we have good reason to believe that the behavioral data under study are also normally distributed, it is appropriate to assess an individual score with reference to that population pattern. Such comparison of an individual to the normal population requires that we know how far the individual score is from the mean, in standard deviation units.

This question can be answered by a very simple arithmetic manipulation: Subtract the mean from the score and divide by the standard deviation. The result is called the z-score (a standardized score), and the shorthand method, or formula, looks like this:

> **The Standard Score**
>
> $$z = \left\{ \frac{\text{Raw Score} - \overline{X} \text{ of the Population}}{\text{Standard Deviation of the Population}} \right\}$$

If the raw score happens to be smaller than the mean, the numerator and, hence, the z-score, is a negative value. Using the normal distribution chart, your instructor will show you how z-scores (and others) distribute within the population. Percentile scores can also be understood better from the normal distribution chart, and they can be compared to z-scores. It is the standard deviation, which was so laboriously calculated, that allows the scientist to relate individual scores to the normal distribution and hence to the population.

4.5

You have surely encountered at some time an instance where a measure of human behavior was given to you but was not interpreted. Perhaps you were given a score on a classroom test and felt disappointed or even frustrated because you did not know how you compared to others. On the other hand, if you were given a physical measure, such as height, you would not feel the same way. Why not?

A raw score, such as a test result or the score you obtained in Project 2, is almost meaningless until it is evaluated. You might get a rough idea of where you stand by asking some friends how they did, but this strategy is far from precise. This problem results from the nature of the scales used in behavioral quantification.

Psychologists usually compare data to **norms** in order to interpret behavioral scores, and the reference is either the entire set of data or a measure of central tendency. It is interesting to note that even a physical measure like height is more meaningful if it is interpreted against norms. For example, a man of 5'9" is close to average in height. But what if you found out that he was on a professional basketball team, or that he was a Scandinavian? What if he was a race horse jockey, or a Japanese by birth? Would the label "average" still apply if you had this norm information?

Principles of Statistical Inference

The Normal Curve

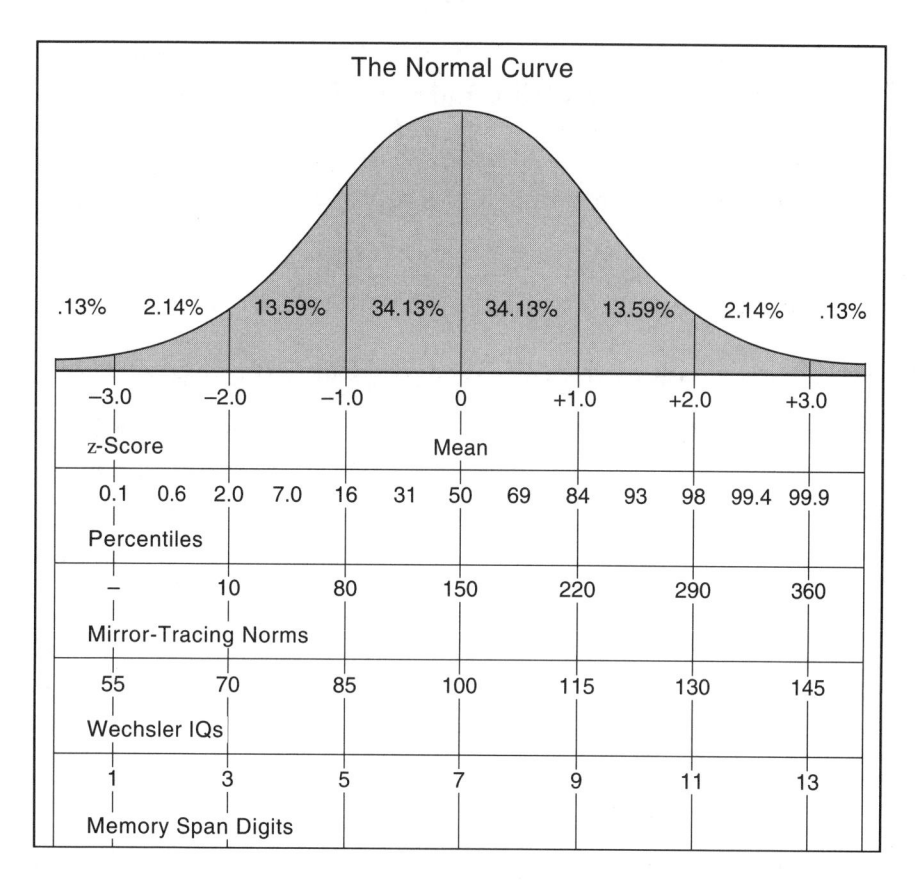

z-Score	−3.0	−2.0	−1.0	0 (Mean)	+1.0	+2.0	+3.0
Area %	.13%	2.14%	13.59%	34.13% / 34.13%	13.59%	2.14%	.13%
Percentiles	0.1	0.6 2.0 7.0	16 31	50	69 84	93 98 99.4	99.9
Mirror-Tracing Norms	—	10	80	150	220	290	360
Wechsler IQs	55	70	85	100	115	130	145
Memory Span Digits	1	3	5	7	9	11	13

5. INTERPRETATION

The following questions are for discussion, study, and review.

A. Define each of the following terms introduced in this study: sample, population, inferential statistics, standard deviation, observed difference, significant difference, level of confidence, experimental hypothesis, null hypothesis, Rosenthal effect, standard score.

B. How would you explain the logic of a statistical test of significance to a person who had not studied the subject?

C. Sometimes you hear a reference to the "reliability" of a statistical measure such as a difference between means. Just what does this mean when applied to the data of this experiment and how does it relate to "tests of significance"?

D. When we read in a newspaper that something is greater than something else ("rainfall is more this year," "school children are smarter than their parents were," "mental illness is on the increase," "sex deviance is more prevalent now"), what else should we look for before we accept it as a fact?

E. What is the importance of the fact that behavior, when measured carefully, frequently fits the pattern of the normal curve?

F. What is meant by the **validity** and **reliability** of a psychological test?

Principles of Statistical Inference 55

Student _____ Section _____ Due Date _____

PRINCIPLES OF STATISTICAL INFERENCE MOTOR LEARNING DATA

1. Write a Results and Discussion section for the Motor Learning experiment of Project 2. Refer to the IRP section for guidelines. Attach Tables 3-1 and 3-2.

2. To complete the next project, Project 4, we need to collect data on an eye–hand coordination task called the Pursuit Rotor. Use the Pursuit Rotor experiment file. Run six trials on yourself as subject and calculate the mean score. In this case, a score should represent time on target. (By the way, good tail gunners on World War II bombers averaged better than 18 out of 20 seconds on target!) Complete Table 3-3 in this project.

Principles of Statistical Inference

TABLE 3-1

SIGN TEST OF THE EFFECTS OF QUIET AND DISTRACTION ON MOTOR LEARNING

Subject No.	Mirror Tracing Quiet Average Score	Mirror Tracing Distracted Average Score	Sign
1.			
2.			
3.			
4.			
5.			
6.			
7.			
8.			
9.			
10.			
11.			
12.			
13.			
14.			
15.			
16.			
17.			
18.			
19.			
20.			
Significance Level $p <$		Total Number of Plus Signs	

Principles of Statistical Inference

TABLE 3-2

ASSESSMENT OF INDIVIDUAL MIRROR-TRACING SCORES

Standardized Mirror-Tracing Scores		
	Quiet Score	Distracted Score
Your individual or raw score		
z-score using the $\overline{X}$ and standard deviation from the normal curve		
Percentile rank interpolated from the normal curve		

TABLE 3-3

PURSUIT ROTOR PERFORMANCE

Pursuit Rotor Performance		
Run the Motor Skills experiment file "Pursuit Rotor"		
Trial	Score	
1.		
2.		
3.		
4		
5.		
6.		
$\overline{X} =$		

PROJECT 4

OPTIMIZING SKILL ACQUISITION

In school psychology, as in athletic performance, childhood development, language learning, and other areas, there are optimum conditions for sequencing and scheduling learning. For example, sleep facilitates memory consolidation, so, for college students, getting some sleep is preferable to all-night cramming. In **state-dependent learning**, retention is best if it occurs in the same physical or environmental condition as the original learning. Thus you will do better if you learn without drugs, even coffee, and then, for example, take a test nondrugged. In this project we investigate another important factor: the distribution of practice effect. What optimum spacing between trials in learning acquisition will adequately promote learning while at the same time permit the dissipation of negative effects such as fatigue, stress, or anxiety? Of course, many factors can affect your ability to develop skills. Innate ability is one, but you cannot do much to change that. **Motivation** is another. Many self-help and other programs have been designed to help us manipulate our motivation. Interestingly, you can have too much motivation, which is detrimental to performance, as well as have too little motivation, which is more common. In other words, there is an optimum level of motivation for particular tasks.

It would be a mistake to overgeneralize from the results of this experiment on motor learning, but the experiment might stimulate hypotheses about performance optimization that you might consider for your Individual Research Project. For example, is there an optimum distribution for the massing or spacing of learning trials?

In the behavioral sciences, learning is one of the most common dependent variables. But learning itself cannot be directly observed; rather, we look at performance. The problem is similar to that of definition, which was alluded to in the introduction to this section. Generally, when some unobservable phenomenon affecting behavior, like learning, occurs within the organism, it is called an intervening variable. Thus, in observing performance (the overt behavior), we hope to gain information about the **intervening variable** of learning (the covert behavior). Perhaps an example will help clarify this distinction between learning and performance. A child who has learned to spoon-feed himself or herself may go back to the bottle when a younger child is born. Should we say that in such cases the skills are forgotten or unlearned? No, rather, we separate the concepts of learning and performance, observing the latter and inferring the former.

1. Purposes

To determine the differential effect of spacing-out trials vs. massing trials in the development of an eye–hand coordination task. To demonstrate the method of matched groups. To test the effect of a rest period following massed learning.

Optimizing Skill Acquisition

2. APPARATUS

Macintosh computers with the experiment files Pursuit Rotor 2 and Pursuit Rotor 3 created by the Motor Skills application.

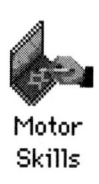

3. PROCEDURE

In many experiments it is not possible to use a **within-subject** counterbalanced design (as we did in Project 2) to help control for the variability that occurs from the fact that we are all different from one another. In this project, we use a **matched-groups** experimental design as another means of handling this problem. The logic of this design is straightforward. If two groups start out the same, but end up different after a manipulation, then we can conclude that the manipulation probably caused the difference.

In this project, the instructor is the experimenter and the students serve as subjects. To prepare for this experiment, you should have your own score on the pursuit rotor test from Project 3. The general design of the study has the class divided into two matched groups. The instructor will do this so the **mean** and **variability** of one-half of the class are equal to those of the other half. One of the two groups will be called the "spaced-learning group" and the other the "massed-learning group." The procedure for operating and scoring is similar to that used in Project 3. However, the two groups will differ in the order in which the trials are taken. Depending on the size of the class, each of the experimental groups may be divided into smaller groups, each with its own Macintosh.

3.1 SPACED LEARNING

Subjects in this group arrange the order in which they practice, and the same order is maintained throughout. The file Pursuit Rotor 2 is started and subject 1 is given one trial (10 seconds). During the following 5-second intertrial interval, subject 1 hands the mouse to subject 2, who is given one trial, and so on. As soon as the last subject finishes, each records his or her data from the Data window. Save the data, then run the next set of trials by choosing **Run** under the **Experiments** menu. Subject 1 must be ready to take the second trial. This procedure is continued without interruption until all subjects in the group have had five trials.

3.2 Massed Learning

The order of subjects in this group is not important, because each subject completes five trials before the next subject has a turn. For each subject, Pursuit Rotor 2 is run for the five trials. After each subject is finished, he or she saves and names the data file or transcribes it to the lab manuals as directed.

For the spaced-learning subjects, the time between trials is 15 seconds times $(N - 1)$; for the massed-learning subjects, the time between trials is 5 seconds. The scores we use are time on-target.

3.3 Retesting

After the data have been collected and analyzed, retest the two groups by giving one more trial to each subject using Pursuit Rotor 3. This can be done by having each person work on his or her own computer. A sign test for each group between trials 5 and 6 will show whether a significant improvement in performance occurred after a rest period.

3.4 Descriptive Analysis of Results

The instructor will direct students in posting all subjects' scores into Table 4-1. Plot two curves (spaced and massed) on the same graph to reveal differences in performance progress.

3.5 Statistical Analysis of Results

Although the curves probably indicate an observed difference between the spaced and massed groups, we want to demonstrate that the difference is statistically significant. In fact, the most convincing evidence would be to demonstrate that the two groups *are not* significantly different on trial 1, but that they *are* significantly different on trial 5. We made an effort to get matched groups by using the scores you obtained on an earlier project, but there is still the question: Did this experimental control actually work? Because no massing or spacing affects performance on trial 1, our experimental manipulation (the independent variable) could not have produced a difference on this trial. Using a test to determine if a manipulation had the desired effect is generally termed a **manipulation check**.

Our task will be to run a test of the difference between groups on trial 1 and a similar test on trial 5. We cannot use the sign test here as we have been doing because there is no reasonable way to decide which subject in the massed group "belongs" with which subject in the spaced group. Recall that in the sign test, the scores from the two groups could be paired, because one subject produced the two scores under two different conditions. Thus, they "belonged" together. In this experiment, the groups are **independent groups**. Can you think of a way we could do the matching process in order to have paired scores and use the sign test? A test of significance appropriate to our present data and almost as easy as the sign test is the **Mann–Whitney U-test**. Perform the following operation, recording your results in Table 4-2.

Step 1. List all the scores from trial 1 in the table under "Score" regardless of the group the score comes from (massed or spaced). Put the *smallest* score at the top and then the next smallest, and so on down to the largest. As you enter the score, put a light check mark in the S or M column, depending on which group that score belongs to.

Step 2. Where there are checks in the S and M columns, enter the rank (from column 1) beside the check in the same column. Watch carefully for ties; when they occur, use the average rank for all tied scores. Find the sum of each column under "Ranks."

Step 3. Subtract the *largest* of the two sums (S or M) from a constant determined by the number of cases in the two groups. This constant has been worked out and is shown in Table 4A for the combination of cases you are likely to encounter. The result is the **U-value**.

Step 4. Compare your U-value with the additional entries in Table 4A for the particular combination of group size you used. If the U-value is *no larger than* the first entry, then the difference is significant at the 5% level; if it is no larger than the second entry, it is significant at the 1% level.

Repeat the analysis on the data for trial 5. Make a sign-test analysis between trials 5 and 6 for each group in Table 4-3.

The logic of the Mann–Whitney U-test should be clear. If the two groups (massed learning and spaced learning, in this case) are really not different, then we would expect the combined rankings in Table 4-2 to show cases from the two groups randomly intermixed. On the other hand, if they were clearly and unequivocally different, we might expect that all of the cases from one group would be ranked before we encountered any of the cases from the other group, or something very close to that pattern. Thus, the degree of overlap in the rankings is the basis for assessing the probability that the two groups are different. As in the sign test, the 1% and the 5% levels of confidence indicate the probability that the results are due to chance. Unlike the sign test, however, the Mann–Whitney U-test can be used in cases where we have no basis for pairing the scores from the two groups—that is, where they are independent.

TABLE 4A

MANN-WHITNEY *U*-TEST OF STATISTICAL SIGNIFICANCE

Sample Size Group A	Sample Size Group B	Constant	5% Level	1% Level
4	4	26	2	0
5	4	30–35*	3	0
5	5	40	4	1
6	5	45–51*	5	2
6	6	57	7	3
7	6	63–70*	9	5
7	7	77	11	6
8	7	84–92*	13	8
8	8	100	16	10
9	8	108–117*	18	11
9	9	126	21	14
10	9	135–145*	24	16
10	10	155	27	19
11	10	165–176*	31	22
11	11	187	34	25
12	11	128–210*	38	28
12	12	222	42	31
13	12	234–247*	47	35
13	13	260	51	39

Column heading note: Subtract the largest sum of ranks from the constant. This result is significant if it is = or < the values below.

* If the largest sum of ranks comes from the largest group, use the larger constant. If the largest sum comes from the smaller group, use the smaller constant.

6. INTERPRETATION

The following questions are for discussion, study, and review.

A. Identify each of the terms introduced in this project: motivation, state-dependent learning, massed learning, spaced learning, Mann–Whitney U-test, U-value, comparison of U-test and sign test, matched-group design, independent groups.

B. Identify the independent variable, the dependent variable, and at least one controlled variable in this experiment.

C. What did you find in your statistical analysis? Make a probability statement about the effect of spaced or massed practice trials.

D. Can you generalize the results of this study to the student practice of cramming? What additional information would you need to know?

E. Can you suggest how this kind of study might be used by an industrial psychologist who is assigned the task of increasing production?

F. What observed difference did you find between trials 5 and 6 for each of the two groups? Was this difference significant? What relation does this finding have to the distinction made between learning and performance? Why was a sign test used?

G. Define massed and spaced learning in terms of this experiment. What type of definition will you use?

Student _____ Section _____ Due Date _____

OPTIMIZING SKILL ACQUISITION

1. Describe your personal study habits. Indicate three things you might do to optimize your performance. Be specific to your personal case.

2. Write a formal Discussion Section for the results your class obtained. Include a graph of your two groups. Refer to the IRP section for guidelines on writing the various parts of scientific communications.

3. Present any additional material requested by your instructor.

4. Include your three tables and the learning curve graph.

TABLE 4-1

TIME ON-TARGET FOR MASSED AND SPACED GROUPS

Subject No.	Trial 1	2	3	4	5	Time Out	6
	Massed-Practice Group						
1.							
2.							
3.							
4.							
5.							
6.							
7.							
8.							
9.							
10.							
	Spaced-Practice Group						
1.							
2.							
3.							
4.							
5.							
6.							
7.							
8.							
9.							
10.							

TABLE 4-2
MANN-WHITNEY *U*-TEST OF MASSED VS. SPACED LEARNING

Combined Rank	Trial 1 Score	Trial 1 Ranks S	Trial 1 Ranks M	Trial 5 Score	Trial 5 Ranks S	Trial 5 Ranks M
1.						
2.						
3.						
4.						
5.						
6.						
7.						
8.						
9.						
10.						
11.						
12.						
13.						
14.						
15.						
16.						
17.						
18.						
19.						
20.						
Σ						
Significance Level	ρ			ρ		

TABLE 4-3

SIGN TEST FOR IMPROVED PERFORMANCE FOLLOWING REST

Subject No.	Trial 6	Trial 5	Sign
	Massed-Practice Group		
1.			
2.			
3.			
4.			
5.			
6.			
7.			
8.			
9.			
10.			
	Significance Level ρ	Total Number of Plus Signs	
	Spaced-Practice Group		
1.			
2.			
3.			
4.			
5.			
6.			
7.			
8.			
9.			
10.			
	Significance Level ρ	Total Number of Plus Signs	

PROJECT 5

PROPOSING YOUR OWN RESEARCH

Creating a specific research proposal in science is important to help clarify both your ideas and your procedures. A proposal that details your step-by-step methodology, subjects, hypothesis, and method of data analysis must also be approved by various ethics reviews as well as by colleagues to make sure the work is appropriate and productive. For our teaching laboratories, your instructor serves as the arbiter for ethics compliance within the guidelines set down by your institution.

Your IRP proposal only needs to be about a page in length, but it must be very specific. Look at the following sample proposal and background library research for a study of the effects of caffeine on motor skills performance. The proposal forms a kind of contract between you and your instructor for what you can and cannot do to satisfy the requirements for your final IRP project, which is described at the back of this manual.

One of the hardest parts initially is to choose a topic and identify a working hypothesis concerning some question of behavior. If you look at other projects in the manual, you will find that some hypotheses are already suggested for you. For example, in the introduction to Project 2, the assertion is made that females perform better than males at mirror tracing. How can you design an experiment to test such an hypothesis?

One source of ideas might be your major, an area where you have some experience. Suppose you are a business major interested in marketing. You might use the application Reaction Time in the *MacLaboratory for Psychology* software to present pictures and collect responses to various corporate logos. Which are most readily recognized? Can you formulate and test new hypotheses about why? Suppose you are a computer science major interested in human interface design. You might use almost the same procedures but instead look at the issue of the recognizability of screen icons. Suppose you are an engineer and want to investigate the best position to display safety or security warnings, as in a nuclear power plant. You could do essentially the same experiment to find the best position, color, size, or location for emergency messages on a screen. The point is to propose a project that is interesting and relevant to you. It must also, of course, be accomplishable within the limitations set by your instructor. If you are still stuck, get some ideas from him or her.

The content of a proposal should clearly state the following: the hypotheses, the independent variables, the dependent variables, the controlled variables, the subjects to be used, the methodology, the expected results, and the type of data analysis.

The following experimental outline concerns the effect of caffeine on arcade game performance. We have provided it here as an example of the process by which a proposal comes into being.

1. Purposes

To help students formalize the statement of an hypothesis and the plan for a research project of their own. To attend to ethical issues and concerns in research. To use the **shareware** arcade game

Proposing Your Own Research 79

Maelstrom, by Andrew Welch, Ian Gilman, and Mark Lewis in the design and execution of a simple sample experiment.

2. APPARATUS

To run the game Maelstrom requires a color Macintosh with at least 4 Mb of RAM. You need to tabulate your data in Table 5-1 and indicate at the top of that table your two conditions for the independent variable.

Maelstrom is a shareware game distributed with your software with the express permission of the author and Ambrosia software. If you decide to keep and use this software, you are ethically obliged to send in your shareware fee as described in the program.

Maelstrom

3. PROCEDURES

For our example proposal and experiment, we look at the effects of caffeine on the type of motor skills (primarily reaction time) involved in arcade game performance. An alternative experiment to run if coffee is unavailable or inappropriate would be to use only your preferred hand for one condition and your nonpreferred hand for the other. Somewhat counterintuitively, there is usually no significant difference between the two hands. Assuming you can use caffeine as an independent variable, the following illustrates some of the main steps you would go through in writing a proposal and conducting the research.

3.1 LIBRARY RESEARCH

Prior to writing your proposal, you need to do library research on your topic. This gives you important background information you may need to conduct a logical and thoughtful piece of research. Remember, your objectives are research that is ethical, manageable, focused, and approved. Unlike other laboratory courses, you will be doing something original and creative, which may cause you to worry about what to do. Your library research can help answer that question. You might also consider how behavioral research might relate to your major. There is no requirement that your research be primarily in psychology.

The following example shows what library research might turn up about caffeine and motor skills.

3.2

This background information on caffeine and motor skills was developed by my colleagues Pauline Nye and Jack Clarkson at the University of Otago, in New Zealand.

Caffeine occurs in plants widely distributed throughout the world. From earliest times, humans have made beverages from aqueous extracts of these plants. Coffee, the seed of *Coffea arabia* and related species, contains caffeine. Tea, the leaves of *Thea sinensis*, contains caffeine and theophylline, and cocoa, obtained from the seed of *Theobroma cacao*, contains caffeine and theobromine. Even some soft drinks, particularly the cola-flavored drinks, contain caffeine, from the nut of the tree *Cola acuminata*. The flavor of coffee and these other drinks depends on a variety of substances, including caffeine.

The earliest history of these drinks is lost in considerable obscurity, the absence of fact being compensated for by a profusion of conjectural statements and mythical stories.

Coffee drinking probably began in Arabia and was certainly popular there by A.D. 900. The habit spread throughout the Islamic world but did not reach Europe until the seventeenth century. Coffee houses were common in England by 1650 and were important meeting places, so much so that Charles II believed they were *"hot-beds of seditious talk and slanderous attacks upon persons in high stations,"* and had them closed; but eleven days later this order was repealed! Charles II was not alone in condemning coffee; in 1674 a group of women in England published a pamphlet entitled "The Women's petition against coffee." Part of it reads:

> *Certainly our Countrymen's palates are becoming as Fanatical as their Brains; how else is't possible they should Apostatise from the good old primitive way of Ale-drinking, to run a Whoreing after such variety of Foreign Liquors, to trifle away their time, scald their Chops, and spend their money, all for a little base, black, thick, nasty, bitter, stinking nauseous Puddle water.*

Earlier in the eighteenth century J. S. Bach wrote the Coffee Cantata to a satirical text by Henrici. A father upbraids his daughter for coffee drinking. He says *"You evil child, you wicked woman! When will you do as you're told? Give up this coffee craze."* He tells her she will have no husband until she gives up coffee, but in the end the girl schemes to get her husband and her coffee. Bach himself adds this ending to the text, *"But when their mothers and grandmothers love to brew coffee, how can their daughters be refused it?"*

Concern about the possible deleterious effects of caffeine has been expressed more recently. In 1909, Coca-Cola manufacturers were accused of putting a "poisonous ingredient"—caffeine—in their product. The company paid for some research into the effects of caffeine, however, reduced the amount, and won their case. There is no evidence that caffeine in moderate amounts is harmful to health.

The making of coffee is an art since the beans must be properly roasted, ground, and cooked. Nowadays, instant coffee is very popular, and although the technique for making it was perfected about 1900, it was not made on a large scale until the 1950s.

Pharmacological effects. Modern pharmacological studies of caffeine amply confirm the ancient belief that coffee has a stimulant action. The average cup of coffee contains between 100 and 150 mg of caffeine, approximately a physiologically effective dose. Naturally, the daily ingestion of even this amount of a potent alkaloid is bound to exert some pharmacological action.

The lethal dose for a person who is not sensitive is 10g (equivalent to 70–100 cups of coffee taken at once). Overindulgence of coffee is harmful and may lead to sleeplessness, restlessness, headaches, and irregularities of the heart beat.

People do develop **pharmacological tolerance**, because a single 150-mg dose of coffee does not affect the pulse rate of habitual coffee drinkers (5 or more cups per day), but it elevates that of about 40% of the people who are not habitual coffee drinkers. Habitual drinkers are less likely to report difficulties sleeping than occasional drinkers, and this is presumably because habitual drinkers have developed some tolerance.

Habitual drinkers may report headaches and negative feelings if deprived of coffee for 18 hours. For these people, the headaches disappear and positive feelings return after drinking coffee, but not after taking a **placebo**. Caffeine has several pharmacological actions: It stimulates the central nervous system, acts on the kidney to promote loss of water, stimulates cardiac muscle, and relaxes smooth (involuntary) muscle.

Caffeine is a powerful CNS stimulant. The cortex is affected first, then the medulla; the spinal cord is stimulated only by very large amounts of caffeine. Caffeine stimulates all portions of the cortex. Its main behavioral effect is to produce a more rapid and clearer flow of thought, and to allay drowsiness and fatigue. The CNS stimulating effects of caffeine cannot be increased to a therapeutically useful degree because of cardiovascular side effects. There is surprisingly little good work on the effects of caffeine on perceptual and motor tasks. The findings are often confused or contradictory, and many experiments have not been properly conducted—too few subjects, control subjects not properly matched with experimental subjects, and subjects given only one dose level and one test after one arbitrary time interval. However, the evidence suggests that a wide range of behaviors can be enhanced by caffeine. In some cases caffeine produces superior performance; in other cases it seems only to restore performance that has been degraded by fatigue, boredom, and inattention.

Laboratory experiments suggest that caffeine prolongs the time during which a person can perform physically exhausting work, but the effects of caffeine on reaction time are unclear, with some studies showing improved performance and others debilitated performances.

The effect of caffeine has been assessed on the performance of a variety of tasks involving complex muscular adjustments. Simple tapping tests seem relatively unaffected. Steadiness, however, may deteriorate due to caffeine-induced tremor. Some researchers have wondered if caffeine promotes learning. Some results show improved attention. Others find that caffeine improves the speed of mathematical addition. Chute (1980) reports that stimulation of cyclic AMP by xanthines sometimes found in coffee facilitates memory in animals and humans.

Franks et al. (1975) have investigated the effects of caffeine with and without alcohol on various tasks related to driving skills. Since the abstract of their work is a model of brevity and precision, it is quoted here in full:

The effect of caffeine (300 mg/70 kg) on cognitive, perceptual and motor functions was investigated both alone and in combination with ethanol (0.75 g/kg) in 68 healthy student volunteers of both sexes. A test battery consisting of standing steadiness, simple and choice reaction time, manual dexterity, numerical reasoning, perceptual speed *and verbal fluency was used. Placebos for both drugs were included. Caffeine was administered in decaffeinated coffee immediately after finishing drinking the alcoholic beverage. A peak plasma ethanol concentration of 92 + 4 mg/100 ml occurred at 40 min. which was not modified by caffeine. Caffeine did not antagonize the ethanol-induced decrement in performance except in the reaction time tests. Caffeine alone causes a significant increase in body sway at 40 min.***

3.3 A Sample Proposal

The hypothesis is that 100 mg of caffeine will improve performance on the arcade game Maelstrom. The independent variable is the presence or absence of caffeine. This is arranged by using a cup of either regular or decaffeinated instant coffee in a double-blind experimental design. The dependent variable is the scores on three trials of the arcade game. Random assignment to one of two groups (caffeinated and decaffeinated) has to be used because the effects of caffeine last too long for a within-subjects design. Controlled variables are equivalent age and demographics, and equivalent prior learning on the task (random assignment and manipulation checked). All subjects will be requested to have had similar meals, no caffeinated beverages, and so forth prior to participating. The two types of coffee (coded A and B) will be served the same way for all subjects, as sugar affects caffeine soluability. The actual levels of caffeine estimated from the caffeine concentration of popular brands are about 100 mg for three level spoonfuls of regular caffeinated coffee and about 6 mg for a similar amount of decaffeinated coffee. One hundred milligrams is apparently a physiologically effective dose, one to two hours after consumption, since it has been reported to increase performance on motor skills tasks. Coffee will be served at the very beginning of lab and testing will begin about one-half hour later, after the discussion of proposal writing. The predicted result is that caffeine will improve performance on Maelstrom compared to no caffeine. A Mann–Whitney U-test will be employed to test for significance of any observed differences on trial 1 and on overall scores.

---

*Franks, H. M., Hagedorn, H., Hensley, V. R., Hensley, W. J. and G. A. Starmer. (1975) The effect of caffeine on human performance, alone and in combination with alcohol. *Psychopharmacologia, 45,* 177–181.

4. Ethical Principles

You will be representing yourselves and your university, and your research must conform to accepted standards of ethical and professional conduct in experimentation. Your department and institution may require that you be approved by an Institutional Review Board (IRB) in addition to being approved by your instructor. It is *your* responsibility to make sure you comply with all requirements. There are a number of guiding principles to which you must adhere.

4.1 Risks/Benefit Ratio

In research with human or animal subjects, any risks must be clearly outweighed by the potential benefits of the research. Because it is unlikely that a significant benefit will come directly from this project, the risks involved with your research *have* to be nil. This then excludes projects involving prescription or illegal drugs, alcohol, sexuality, money, psychological or physical stress, pain, and social or personal discomfort. There can be no deception of any kind involved with the project.

4.2 Informed Consent

Any participant in your experiment must be fully informed as to the nature, purpose, and design of the experiment. They must know precisely what they will be asked to do. They must *volunteer* without any form of coercion or social pressure. In fact, the best arrangement is to recruit other class members or personal friends to participate in your project. As a general rule, instructors will not approve proposals that require a large number of subjects.

4.3 Voluntary Withdrawal

Subjects must be told clearly that they may stop participating at any point in an experiment for any reason. There must be no penalties whatsoever attached to voluntary withdrawal.

4.4 Anonymity

Subjects must be told clearly that their privacy and anonymity will be protected, and they must be told the means you will employ to ensure this.

Proposing Your Own Research

4.5 ETHICS

Always be ethical. Ethics is not just something you should arbitrarily apply to experiments. For example, if you use the Maelstrom software on your own computer, in a dorm or after this class, send in your shareware fee.

5. APPROVAL AND EXECUTION

After discussing the proposal, and its approval, and planning for its execution, you may go ahead and collect and analyze your data.

If your class and/or instructor do not approve of the caffeine study, you may want to try an alternative study: testing the effects of handedness on arcade game performance. Use a within-subjects **Latin square** design, where half the class starts with three trials of their preferred hand and half starts with their nonpreferred hand. Switch hands for three more trials. Table 5-1 can serve for data collection. Extra sign test and Mann-Whitney *U*-test tables are at the back of the laboratory manual.

6. DATA SUMMARY

The class should discuss how to present the results for this project.

7. INTERPRETATION

The following questions are for discussion, study, and review.

A. What were some of the behavioral experiments that caused professional societies like the American Psychological Association to codify ethical standards and principles?

B. What is the difference between an experiment and a naturalistic observation? Both types of research can be used for your IRP.

C. What factors were not controlled in the experiment? How could the experiment be improved?

D. Can you think of two or three hypotheses that deal with arcade games or associated behavior that might form the basis for your Individual Research Project?

Proposing Your Own Research 87

Student _____ Section _____ Due Date _____

Research Proposal:
Maelstrom

1. Write your Results section of this project.

2. Write an abstract explaining what was done in this project and what your conclusions are, based on the results.

3. Attach a discussion draft of your IRP Proposal.

4. Attach Table 5-1 and your other tables and graphs associated with the project.

5. Enter your average Maelstrom score now in Table 9-3 of Project 9.

TABLE 5-1

ARCADE GAME PERFORMANCE

| Sub-ject No. | Independent Variable ||||||||
| | Trial Score |||| Trial Score ||||
	1	2	3	Total	1	2	3	Total
1.								
2.								
3.								
4.								
5.								
6.								
7.								
8.								
9.								
10.								
11.								
12.								
13.								
14.								
15.								
16.								
17.								
18.								
19.								
20.								
				$\bar{X} =$				$\bar{X} =$

INTRODUCTION

SECTION 2

BEHAVIORAL NEUROSCIENCES

Section 2 Behavioral Neurosciences

The behavioral neurosciences study the physical and mental functions of the brain using techniques ranging from microscopic to macroscopic, molecular to molar, cellular to whole organism. Although not all philosophical issues of mind and brain are, or can be, resolved the neuroscientist functions with the understanding that mind and brain are one and the same thing. The creative, imaginative, learning, thinking, emotive "mind" is but an expression of the physical structure of the brain.

The relationship between psychological events and the activity of the brain is one of the most interesting areas of psychology. It answers the "why" and "what" questions that affect students' everyday lives. Why do drugs and alcohol have the effect they do? What characteristic sex differences are found in the brain? What changes in your brain when you learn something? What physical change occurs in the brain to people suffering from **Alzheimer's disease**? Why am I depressed? In the neurosciences, answers to such questions are found on several levels; they may be molecular—for example, a change in **neurotransmitters** and their **receptors**—or they may be molar—for example, learning or motivation—and so on.

Just asking the right questions can open whole avenues of research. For example, Dr. Solomon Snyder wondered why the human brain should be so uniquely sensitive to an extract of the poppy plant (morphine). He hypothesized that perhaps an endogenous morphine-like substance already existed in our brains

Introduction

(**endorphine**). This proved to be the case, and Dr. Snyder had the foresight, determination, and ability to demonstrate it. In the process, he discovered a whole new class of neurotransmitters and opiate receptors.

The process of asking questions and finding answers in the behavioral neurosciences sometimes challenges our view of the brain as an inviolate organ—and sometimes challenges societal values. For example, in the management of **Parkinson's disease**, is the explanting of **dopaminergic** fetal brain tissue a socially acceptable as well as viable mechanism of treatment? What moral and ethical considerations need to be addressed? One accepted treatment for uncontrollable epilepsy with severe seizures is to split the brain by severing the interconnecting fibers of the **corpus collosum**. This usually prevents the recruitment of other parts of the brain, providing a measure of relief from seizures. But what behavioral side effects can you expect from such a procedure?

In the 1930s and 1940s, frontal lobotomies were commonly used to control aggressive or emotional problems and the behavior of schizophrenics. Although the picklike instruments that used to be inserted above the eye and pushed into the anterior pole of the frontal lobe were eventually replaced by more civilized and "high-tech" cryogenic probes, was the procedure itself justifiable? About 18,000 frontal lobotomies were carried out, and, as predicted from earlier research on primates, the flattening of emotions was accompanied by profound loss of executive function, personality changes, and an absence of the motivation and intellectual functions that we identify as being essential to human quality of life. Frontal lobotomies continued to be done as long as they were, at least in part, because the surgeons doing the procedures "fudged" the data concerning their outcome. With the introduction of the major tranquilizers like **chlorpromazine** in the 1950s, a somewhat better pharmacological management of severely aggressive behaviors was achieved than the ultimate political incorrectness of "stirring brains with sharp spoons."

MacLaboratory has been used in many different ways at all levels of research in the behavioral neurosciences. At the molecular level, an example is the experiment file Nictitating Conditioning, run by the application Controller. This represents a system that was used to bring about the learning of a classically conditioned eyeblink response in rabbits. The **cerebellum** is the structure that mediates the paired association of the **unconditional stimulus**, an air puff or mild shock that causes an animal to blink, and the **conditional stimulus**, a tone. Eventually the tone alone **elicits** the response; this is similar to the **classical conditioning** of Pavlov's dog. This bit of learning is of particular interest to the neuroscientist because half of the cerebellum can be trained while the other half can serve as a control, adding to the experiment the power of a **within-subjects design** and causing potentially confounding factors such as intelligence, fear, or amount of sleep to be the same for both the experimental and the learning conditions. The cerebellum of such a trained animal can be put into liquid nitrogen to freeze the biochemical processes and an analysis made of the differences between the trained and untrained side. Because of the within-subject design, differences can logically be assumed to be due to the pairing of the conditional and unconditional stimuli. In other words, we can discover some of the biological changes that occur in cells that have participated in learning. By the way, such changes occur in a group of membrane-bound proteins called **phosphoglycoproteins**. Phosphoglycoproteins probably control the "gates" for the flow of important ions like calcium through the pores of the cell membrane. The **phosporylation state** of these proteins also controls other functions such as **receptor binding affinities**.

At a more molar research level, *MacLaboratory* software has been used like a **tachistoscope**, to present information to one hemisphere of the brain or the other in intact humans. For example, in Project 7, you will investigate whether your left hemisphere processes verbal material better and whether your right hemisphere processes pictographic material better. Clinically, the software application Reaction Time has been used with patients undergoing brain surgery for relief from seizure disorders. In these cases the surgeon wants to avoid primary speech areas and higher level language functions. The software is used to present different types of language stimuli to the awake patient while the psychologist advises the surgeon which areas to avoid.

In neuropsychology, tests of memory, reaction, time, motor skills, and so forth are given to patients with various neurological disorders. Such tests help develop rehabilitation plans or point up difficulties in intellectual functioning that may prove problematic for activities of everyday living. The application Neuropsychology presents some general relationships between the larger structures of the human brain and specific behaviors. Most

Introduction

of these have been derived from a type of research that is sometimes called the "replicated case study." Although probably no two cases of brain injury are identical, there are often enough similarities that you can make fairly accurate predictions if you know the nature and extent of damage and its behavioral consequences.

PROJECT 6
THE BRAIN: STRUCTURE AND FUNCTION

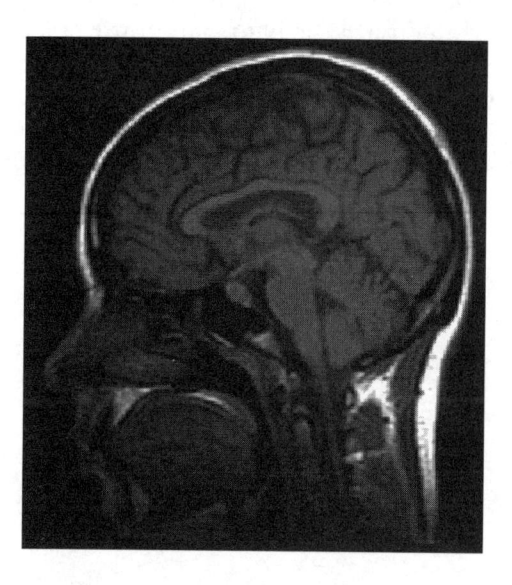

A number of new technologies have emerged to help us visualize the central nervous system. The **CAT scan**, or computed axial tomograph, takes a series of X rays from different angles. A computer then averages these different views to build up a picture of the subtle variations in the radio-opaque densities of different brain structures or lesions within the brain. Before the invention of the CAT scan, the most accurate way of predicting the location of damage within the brain was through behavioral and neuropsychological testing. Although scanning technologies are now better at revealing abnormalities in the structure or activity of the brain, they nevertheless do not address the critical issue of behavioral function. A **neuropsychological assessment** is still the best protocol for predicting whether someone with a disorder of the central nervous system is likely to have difficulties with memory, attention, or other factors that affect the performance of everyday living tasks.

The picture below shows a **mid-saggital** view of the head as seen by an **MRI scan**. The MRI, or magnetic resonance image, is like an axial tomograph, but instead of X rays taken from different angles, magnetic fields are used to detect variations in the way hydrogen atoms are bound by different tissues. The resulting images are high resolution and appear almost like photographs of the inside of the living brain.

This mid-saggital view reveals some of the major structures of the **brain stem** and **diencephalon**. In the *MacLaboratory* software Neuropsychology, you will explore the structural and functional relationships of such midline brain regions.

Images from a CAT scan and MRI do not show the levels of metabolic activity that occur in the brain. To observe which brain regions are activated by particular tasks, with particular syndromes, or with particular behaviors, you can measure regional cerebral blood flow or the uptake of glucose, for example. Some of our former students—Terry Shaw, David Stumpf, George Vroulis, Lynn Harper Mosely, and others—have pioneered in such studies. Basically, a short half-life, radio-labeled substance is injected and scanners surrounding the brain pick up emissions. The movies associated with the Neuroanatomy stack in your software illustrate some of the basic principles of **SPECT** (single positron emission computed tomography) images. These were created using technology developed by Dr. Carl Fristrom and his associates at Strichman Medical Equipment of Medfield, MA.

The Brain: Structure and Function

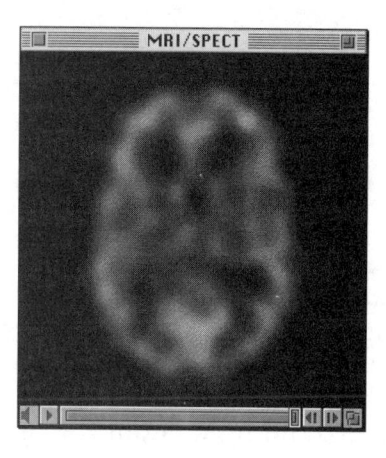

Although the resolution of SPECT images is not as fine as those of MRI, they have the advantage of showing the metabolic activity that may be occurring, or not occurring, and thus indicate the dynamic relationships between neuroanatomy and behavior. The **horizontal section** shown below illustrates that the **gray matter** consisting of cell bodies has higher activity than the **white matter** regions, which consist mostly of fiber pathways. The **lateral ventricles** of the brain contain no cells, and thus show no activity.

Imaging, neuropsychological testing, and traditional neuroanatomical studies have helped us understand the role of cortical regions in human behaviors. Although no one-to-one relationship exists between a particular neuron and a particular behavior, we can say that large cortical regions are major participants or organizers in complex behaviors. With your software, you should be able to learn the major lobes of the **cerebral cortex** and the functions associated with them.

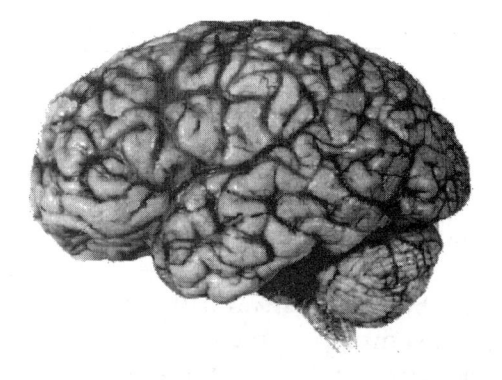

1. PURPOSES

To illustrate the role of the brain in behavior. To utilize a self-paced Macintosh tutorial of basic neuropsychological relationships in the brain.

2. PROCEDURES

The Neuropsychology tutorial includes four different "maps" of the brain, illustrating the cortex of each hemisphere, subcortical structures, and the limbic system. Various pathologies of the brain and identification of how abnormalities affect behavior form the framework for understanding anatomical structure and brain–behavior relationships. This type of work is typically performed by neuropsychologists, whose major responsibilities include diagnosis and rehabilitation of abnormal brain function.

3. INTERPRETATION

The following questions are for discussion, study, and review.

A. Identify each of the following: the anatomical structures of the brain illustrated in the software, the major pathologies of the brain mentioned, and the major structural and behavioral relationships of the CNS.

B. By what process do "correct" connections develop in the CNS? Why do so many neuronal cells die during development?

C. Where is memory in the brain?

D. What physically happens when a brain learns new information? Are new connections made? Are existing connections strengthened? What biochemical events occur within a neuron?

E. Some recovery does seem to occur following brain damage. How is this **plasticity brought** about? What experimental procedures have been used to promote regrowth?

F. What role might diet play in altering neurotransmitter levels? Can diet, for example, increase acetylcholine in the CNS? Would this benefit such pathologies as **Alzheimer's disease**?

The Brain: Structure and Function

G. What role can new experience play in the recovery of functions? How can the microcomputer aid in such rehabilitation?

H. Identify the major structures of the limbic system. What is their role in behavior?

I. What are the different types of aphasia? What structures are responsible?

J. How is neuropsychology different from phrenology?

K. Research a drug addiction. How does the particular drug you've studied affect the brain?

L. What is hemispheric laterality? In what ways do brain hemispheres differ? What effect does gender or handedness have?

M. Using information from the text, lecture, software and/or journal articles, describe the anatomical boundaries of the frontal, temporal, and parietal lobes of the brain. Indicate the major functions of each.

N. Describe the physical process by which CAT, MRI, PET, and SPECT images are created.

The Brain: Structure and Function

Student _____ Section _____ Due Date _____

THE BRAIN: STRUCTURE AND FUNCTION

1. Write an answer for question ___ from the Interpretation section of this project.

2. Print a copy of each of the brain "maps" from the Neuropsychology software, or use the electronic copies in the Experiments section of the Neuroanatomy stack. Label the following: **amygdala, angular gyrus, Broca's area, caudate, cerebellum, corpus callosum, fissure of Rolando, fourth ventricle, hippocampus, hypo-thalamus, motor strip, pituitary gland (hypophysis), massa intermedia, pons, pre-cuneate gyrus, primary somato-sensory cortex, pyriform cortex, reticular formation, septum, sylvian fissure, supra-chiasmatic nucleus, thalamus, Wernicke's area**, and any additional regions or structures required by your instructor.

PROJECT 7

MEASURING HEMISPHERIC SPECIALIZATION

Clinical data suggest that the two hemispheres of the cerebral cortex are somewhat specialized in their function. For most right-handed people, the left hemisphere processes complex verbal and language-related material, and the right hemisphere processes complex perceptual and spatial patterns such as visual symbols or music. The brains of most left-handed individuals also have this pattern of hemispheric specialization, although few left-handers have language and pattern recognition more bilaterally represented, and a very few (about 2%) have specialization reversed from the usual.

On the issue of handedness, it is important that the psychologist not be influenced by cultural prejudice. For example, "dexterous"

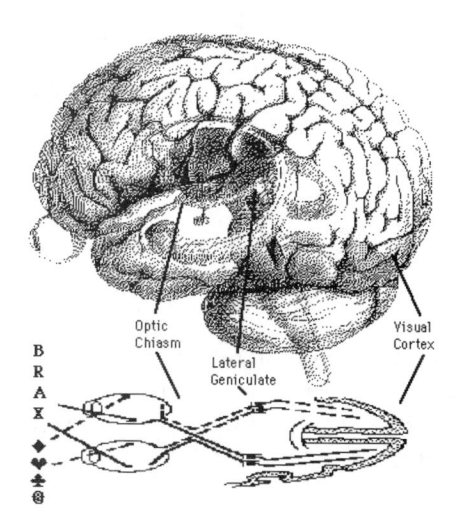

comes from the Latin root word for right, and "sinister" comes from the root word for left. An interesting discussion of this problem is found in an article by Dr. Michael Corballis (Corballis, M. Laterality and Myth, *American Psychologist*, 1980). Use **Psychological Abstracts** to get the exact reference, and find and read this article. In normal individuals, the laterality of cerebral function is not an all-or-none phenomenon. Some language—for example, concrete nouns—seems to be available to the right hemisphere. Normal intercommunication between hemispheres also occurs through the major connecting fibers of the **corpus callosum** and the commisures.

In cases of intractable epilepsy, the interconnections between the hemispheres are sometimes surgically severed. In these patients, it was discovered that each hemisphere had some areas of specialization. In general, we might characterize the left hemisphere as having a facility for detail but not the overall "picture," whereas the right hemisphere has the opposite facility. We can observe aspects of hemispheric specialization in normal individuals because of the organization of the visual system.

All optic fibers originating in the left half of each eye (hemiretina) terminate in the left hemisphere; all fibers that originate in the right hemiretinae terminate in the right hemisphere. Thus, if we control the location in the visual field in which the stimulus is presented, we can determine the hemisphere that receives the visual input. Because visual rays cross over, visual information presented in the right visual field falls on the left hemiretina, and therefore is transmitted to the left hemisphere, whereas visual information presented in the left visual field falls on the right hemiretina and is transmitted to the right hemisphere.

Of potential interest to you for your IRP might be observations that males show more pronounced lateralization of function, females show language superiority, or engineers show spatial relations superiority.

1. Purposes

To demonstrate verbal specialization in the left cerebral hemisphere and symbolic specialization in the right cerebral hemisphere. To illustrate a serial position effect. To illustrate the blind spot in each visual field.

2. APPARATUS

Macintosh computer with the application Hemispheres and the experiment file Cerebral Specialization

3. PROCEDURE

This experiment is designed to demonstrate the differential functioning of the two halves of the brain using a perceptual task. Verbal materials (letters of the alphabet) and symbolic patterns are presented to either the left or right hemisphere for identification. In this project it is important to position the eyes so that the stimuli fall in the correct hemiretina. This can be done by having subjects maintain their fixation on a central target and presenting stimuli on either the right or left side. Stimuli presented far enough to the right will be seen by the left hemiretina and will, therefore, be processed first by the left hemisphere. Stimuli presented far enough on the left will go first to the right hemisphere. By presenting the stimuli for only a very brief time (250 ms) it is assumed that there will not be sufficient duration to allow for complete processing by the other hemisphere using the callosal interconnection.

The distance the eyes are away from the Macintosh screen can also produce variability between subjects in this experiment. Accordingly, we can position the **blind spot** of each eye in order to locate the head at the correct distance. In each eye, the exit point of the optic nerve and the blood vessels contains no visual receptors. We normally do not notice this blind spot because of the overlap of the two visual fields and because of a normal interpolative process of the brain itself.

In this experiment, you will see groups of letters or symbols located either to the left or right of a fixation point. As soon as the stimulus is presented, there is a tendency to move the eyes to fixate on the letters. This occurs automatically because acuity is optimal when you are fixated and focused on a stimulus. Stimulus information on which you are focused is transmitted to both hemispheres. This part of the retina is called the **fovea centralis.** Although the brief presentation of stimuli should minimize your ability to look at or focus on them, you should try nevertheless to keep your eyes on the fixation point. To help maintain your position, use a chin rest—even a conveniently sized pile of books located at the correct distance from the screen will do. (This puts you in a somewhat comical position, but such are the tribulations of science.)

The primary question is whether more letters will be correctly identified when they are presented in the right visual field (and therefore transmitted directly to the left hemisphere) than when they are presented in the left visual field. In the latter case, the information must be relayed from the right hemisphere to the left via the corpus collosum, where signal decay may occur. Similarly, for symbolic material presented to the right hemisphere, we would predict a higher recognition rate.

For left-handed people, the situation is much more individual, but, for the purposes of demonstration, let's assume they tend to have language more highly represented in the right hemisphere.

Thus, in our experiment, the stimuli for left-handed people are presented to the opposite side from that for right handers. In fact, most left-handed individuals seem to have primary left hemisphere language functions. Tests like this and the **Wada technique** show the weakness of our current assumption. Perhaps you might investigate this in an IRP.

The design of the experiment is as follows: On each trial, you focus on the fixation point on the screen. The stimuli is presented when you "click down" on the mouse button to signal you are ready. The visual presentation contains either four letters of the alphabet or four members from the symbol set. You use the mouse to enter your response after each trial by clicking in either the letters you think you saw or the symbols you could identify. Use the "shift key" to match capitalization or find appropriate symbols.

You should recognize this task as one that requires **recognition** of the stimuli. Further, we might observe a phenomenon of memory similar to a **serial position effect**, where the first and last items in the stimulus set might be recalled more accurately than the middle items. One confounding variable here might be the normal scan (from left to right) that characterizes the well-trained Western reading style. Would vertical presentation of stimuli affect the result? How would other cultures that read in a different direction perform? What about written languages that use pictographic or symbolic writing—for example, the difference between **Kanji** and **Kani** verbal representations in Japanese?

Such questions may be the basis for a hypothesis for your Individual Research Project. The application is set up so that you can edit an experiment to use the keyboard to enter data or word descriptions of symbols. This would be a test of **recall**; the difference between recall and recognition performance might be another experiment you could perform. By changing the delay values in the timing dialog box to a longer interval, you might investigate the rate of memory decay. Further investigation of left handedness and cerebral specialization might also be done. Another experiment you could do might be to investigate the role of organization in the recognition of verbal material. Is the number of letters that can be identified affected by the order in which they appear? To examine the question, the letters you program to be presented on the screen can either be randomly arranged (e.g., BXRA) or can follow the regular rules of English orthography (e.g., BRAX) like the stimuli in this project.

4. Data Collection

Using yourself as a subject, collect personal data using the Cerebral Specialization experiment file. In Table 7-1, organize the data from the data window so that you can calculate the number of correct identifications for each task, either letters or symbols, for each of the serial positions in the sets.

5. Data Analysis

The bottom of Table 7-1 summarizes the number of correct identifications for verbal stimuli in the left visual field (LVF) and right visual field (RVF) and similarly for symbol stimuli. Table 7-2 uses class data to determine if there is significant hemispheric specialization for the two different types of stimuli. Notice that the symbol stimuli are much more difficult, but this should not affect your ability to analyze or interpret results.

6. Interpretation

The following questions are for discussion and review.

A. Identify or define: laterality, cerebral asymmetry, hemiretina, blind spot, fovea centralis, optic chiasma, cortical projection areas for vision, Kani and Kanji orthography, corpus callosum, the effect of handedness on asymmetry.

B. If damage occurs to the left hemisphere of a right-handed individual, how might some language function be restored? What are Bliss symbols? Look up the following reference in the APA journal *Neuropsychology* to see how a computer can be used for people with expressive aphasias: Chute, D. L., Conn, G., Dipasquale, M. C., & Hoag, M. (1988). Prosthesis-Ware: A new class of software supporting the activities of daily living. *Neuropsychology, 2,* 41-57.

C. Why would hemispheric specialization evolve in humans? Do any other animals show a similar effect?

D. How has cultural prejudice affected our perception of brain function? Is one hemisphere really dominant over the other?

E. Do people with callosal transections for treatment of epilepsy have split personalities?

F. Women tend to develop earlier and have greater facility with language skills; men with mechanical and spatial skills. Do these differences reflect underlying degrees of laterality in the brain? Are they genetically or hormonally determined? How could this be tested empirically?

G. The icons used on Macintosh routines might be processed by either the right or left hemispheres. How would an industrial or engineering psychologist determine which? What effect might that have on the use of the Macintosh?

Student _____ Section _____ Due Date _____

MEASURING HEMISPHERIC SPECIALIZATION

1. Write an answer for question ___ from the Interpretation section of this project.

2. State a testable hypothesis suggested by this project. Write a Methods section as if from a journal article to describe the stimuli, procedures, and data analysis you would use to evaluate the hypothesis.

3. Using correct APA referencing format (see the Individual Research Project), list the reference for the Corballis (1980) paper.

4. Include the two tables.

TABLE 7-1

THE SERIAL POSITION EFFECT IN RECALL

Verbal Stimuli								Symbol Stimuli							
Right Visual Field				Left Visual Field				Right Visual Field				Left Visual Field			
Serial Position				Serial Position				Serial Position				Serial Position			
1	2	3	4	1	2	3	4	1	2	3	4	1	2	3	4

Totals

$\Sigma =$ $\Sigma =$ $\Sigma =$ $\Sigma =$

TABLE 7-2

TYPE OF STIMULUS AND HEMISPHERIC SPECIALIZATION

Sub-ject No.	Verbal Stimuli				Symbol Stimuli			
	Visual Field		Hand	Sign	Visual Field		Hand	Sign
	Right	Left			Left	Right		
1.								
2.								
3.								
4.								
5.								
6.								
7.								
8.								
9.								
10.								
11.								
12.								
13.								
14.								
15.								
16.								
17.								
18.								
19.								
20.								
	Total No. of Plus Signs				Total No. of Plus Signs			
	Significance Level			ρ	Significance Level			ρ

INTRODUCTION

SECTION 3
COGNITIVE SCIENCES

The cognitive sciences, as defined by Ulric Neisser, "refer to all processes by which the sensory input is transformed, reduced, elaborated, stored, recovered, and used." Neisser's definition reflects how psychologists study human cognition. Cognition begins with an outside stimulus that is actively transformed into an internal cognitive construct. This construct involves reduction or elaboration, not passive registration of surrounding stimuli.

Sensory memory, **short-term memory**, and **long-term memory** are studied as information storage and retrieval processes. How and where are memories stored? Why is there both a long- and a short-term memory? How can I improve my memory? Have you ever encountered the "tip of the tongue" phenomenon where you can almost, but not quite, remember a fact or name? Sometime later (it usually seems to be too late), it "comes to you." Obviously, you stored the fact or name, but there was an immediate problem of retrieval of that information. Why does the retrieval problem exist? What does it tell us about the organization of the brain? One way psychologists study such questions is to measure reaction time. For example, in asking how memory is organized in the brain, you might expect shorter reaction times as you scan your memory and move from one related topic, concept, or word to another. You might expect longer reaction times as you move between unrelated concepts. In general, your hunches here are correct that information is stored in the brain in meaningful groupings. It shows that our brains are not organized like the hard disk of a computer, where information is stored in any available sector. Rather, the human brain puts information together in groupings of interrelated items. The *MacLaboratory* stack Memory illustrates some of these organizational principles.

After information has been received by the brain and stored, it is then accessed and put to use, making decisions and solving problems. Decision making and problem solving are not limited to humans, but we seem better at it for a wider variety of cognitive tasks than other species. Although the average North American chickadee would beat you at its little game of seed hiding and finding in the forest, most cognitive psychologists regard our flexible and generalized ability to problem solve as the most characteristically human activity.

Much research and thought has been given to improving our problem-solving capabilities. Because there is a plethora of dif-

Introduction

ferent problem types, problem solving is broken down into three classifications based on the knowledge and/or skill required to solve the problem. The three are referred to as arrangement problems, rearrangement or induced structure problems, and transformation problems. Each type may exist separately or as a combination problem type. In pure arrangement problems, one is required to arrange the elements of the problem to meet a specific criterion. In rearrangement or induced structure problems, the discovery of the relationship between the elements is the task. Transformation problems have an initial state, a goal state, and an operations state for transforming the initial into the goal state.

The stack Problem-Solving Strategies introduces some examples of the main impediments people face in solving problems. If we learn to recognize some of these types of impediments, we can improve our problem-solving skills. In addition, new strategies and skills in problem solving can be taught that increase the probability of correctly arriving at a solution. Generally, we go through four steps in problem solving. These include (1) recognizing and understanding the problem, (2) generating a hypothesis, (3) testing the hypothesis, and (4) checking the result. We set up algorithms to test the hypotheses and heuristically reduce the number of options. Four general heuristics for solving problems are means/end analysis, intermediate goals, analogy, and diagram. Note, heuristics may be useful, but they do not guarantee successful solutions; they are general rules that reduce or simplify the number of operations used to solve a problem.

As a researcher's tool kit, *MacLaboratory* provides a number of fundamental capabilities that allow you to investigate cognitive performance. The application Hemispheres acts like a **tachistoscope**, permitting information to be presented to one or the other cerebral hemisphere. The application Problem Solving allows you to present different categories of font-based stimuli and offer varying levels or combinations of **feedback**. The Reaction Time application is perhaps the most powerful and the most versatile. It permits the presentation of a variety of types of stimuli such as sounds, movies, or pictures. Reaction Time provides for a millisecond-accurate collection of responses so you can measure cognitive processes. It has been used in applied and clinical settings to measure such things as astronaut performance or the capabilities of people with various neurological conditions such as Alzheimer's disease. It has also been used to study language, development, mental images, and internal cognitive representations. In business and marketing, Reaction Time is used to test product recognition and investigate preferences. In engineering and computer science, it has been used to test human–machine interactions, speed, and interface design.

Computers have been very useful in the cognitive sciences. For example, connectionist models, artificial intelligence, and expert systems approaches have done much to stimulate theories of human cognitive and neurological function. In turn, our understanding of human thought and memory has also contributed in many ways to computer science—for example, consider fuzzy logic. In Project 12, you will use your spreadsheet to investigate neural modeling.

PROJECT 8

MEASURING SHORT-TERM MEMORY

We typically think of memory as having three interrelated components. **Sensory memory** is a short duration change in sensory receptors and primary sensory systems that register environmental information. If we are paying attention, this information enters a working memory stage called **short-term memory**. Unlike your computer's memory, human short-term memory is very limited. If you were to hear a list of random items read out, you would probably be able to remember only about seven if your **memory span** is average. That would be the equivalent of having a computer with one bit of RAM instead of the usual megabytes. The standard deviation for memory span for random digits, **digit span**, is about 2. Thus, approximately 68% of the population can normally remember only somewhere between five and nine random digits. Short-term memory is labile and perseverative. You may have had the experience of trying to keep a phone number "in your head" by repeating it over and over. If you are interrupted or distracted, it is gone. Short-term memory is time-limited and seldom lasts longer than 30 seconds. With such limited short-term memories, it's a wonder we get on. In fact, the human brain is constantly trying to organize and make sense of its environment. Thus, if you were try to remember this phone number, (408) 375-6414, you might keep the familiar groupings as a way to "chunk" the digits together so that you don't exceed your capacity. **Chunking** is actually an official psychological term that refers to the somewhat automatic process by which our brains try to organize and collect together information. If you are from North America, you might not do as well if we presented the number as 40-83-75-64-14. In some European countries this is the more common organization. Thus, this latter series would be more easily chunked by people from those countries. The telephone number, by the way, is real. It is the fax number for Brooks/Cole, the publisher of your software. I suppose you could use it if you needed to get some technical assistance.

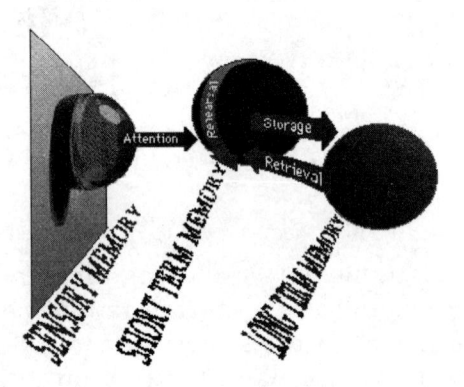

In short-term memory we can observe phenomena that are seen in other types of memory. For example, if you look at the errors made in a list of to-be-remembered digits, the first items and the last items are typically correct. The ones in the middle have the most errors. This is an example of a **primacy-recency effect** similar to that seen in the project on hemispheric specialization. Short-term memory is particularly sensitive to disruption by **interference**.

If you rehearse enough or if information is meaningful or important enough, it eventually enters into **long-term memory**. We have a very large long-term memory capacity, many times larger than the largest computer hard disk. Unlike the computer disk, information is sorted and stored by categories that are "logically related"—at least as far as our brains are concerned. Although reasonably permanent, our long-term memories are not immutable and can change over time. As you might expect, changes usually seem to have the effect of making us feel better about ourselves, making more room by compressing older or less used memories, or modifying or confabulating similar or succeeding events.

Measuring Short-Term Memory

1. Purposes

To measure individual differences in memory span for immediate recall as a measure of short-term memory capacity. To illustrate the effect of "chunking" on short-term memory.

2. Apparatus

Macintosh computer with the application Hemispheres and the experiment file Memory Span.

Hemispheres

3. Procedure

This is a group experiment in which the computer serves as the experimenter and each of the students is a subject. The Memory Span file contains digit and letter-digit stimuli of varying lengths that are randomly mixed. A digit group might be, for example, 7-2-6-1-3, and a letter-digit group might be P-A-L-1-3. Each of these examples contains five units. In the experimental series, the letter-digit groups have been translated from the digit groups through use of the telephone dial code. In the previous example, 7 can be transposed to the letter P, 2 to A, and 6 to L. Thus, if you dialed PAL-13, you would get the same number as if you dialed 7-2613. Our major problem is to determine if these two kinds of code representations are as equivalent to the person dialing as they are to the telephone being dialed.

The different series lengths are presented in random order. After each group of digits or letter-digits is seen, the subject must attempt to recall and enter the group in *exactly the same order as it was seen*. After the entire series has been presented, check under the File Menu with Data Display and score each set in Table 8-1. There are five stimuli of each length. No group is correct unless all the units are given in correct order; there are no extra units.

4. Analysis of Results

Convert each entry in Table 8-1 to a percentage and enter it into the next column. Because there were five trials at each series length, percents will be 0, 20, 40, 60, 80, 100. In order to find that group length which best represents your ability for immediate recall, we use the method of **linear interpolation**. Construct a graph of your own results for digits by plotting group length along the abscissa and percent (0 to 100) along the ordinate. Enter the percent correct figures into the graph and connect them with straight lines to form the "percent correct curve." Now do the same for the percent incorrect figures, which are the converse of the figures you just plotted. Find the point where the two curves cross. If you have secure data, this point will be at or near the 50% point. Drop a vertical line from the crossing point to the abscissa and read your memory span score on that scale. Repeat the procedure for the letter-digit series data using a new graph. If your curves have more than one crossing point, average.

Collect interpolated memory span scores from the entire class and enter these data in Table 8-2. Find the mean for digits and for letter-digits. Draw in these means on your graphs as a vertical line from the appropriate point on the abscissa. This line will be parallel to the interpolation line you drew for your own data, or in rare cases it will overlap. Thus, you can tell if your own memory span is above or below that for the class as a whole.

Again using Table 8-2, apply the sign test to the class data to test the hypothesis. Is the performance on letter-digit series significantly greater than it is for digit series? What does such a test show about "chunking"?

5. INTERPRETATION

The following questions are for discussion, study, and review.

A. As you served in the role of subject in this experiment, what abilities did you feel were being used in performing the task? What is your conclusion regarding short-term memory? What sorts of real-life situations require these abilities?

B. What practical applications do you see as possible for the results of this study? Could you represent the study as an example of engineering psychology?

C. About half of the class will, of necessity, have scores above the class mean and half will have scores below. Just how much information does this give you about your own ability? Would you be satisfied with that kind of information and no more if you were inquiring about your grade on an examination? Memory Span is used in the Wechsler IQ test; how well does it predict IQ?

D. A neuropsychologist often uses memory span in a neurological examination as a ready assessment of a patient's short-term memory. What factors should the neuropsychologist be cautious about before concluding that a low memory span implies faulty short-term memory? Refer also to the normal curve in Project 3.

E. This project contains many control procedures for eliminating or minimizing unwanted variables. Can you identify them? Why did we have several trials, instead of just one at each series length? Why was random order used in the sequence of digits and letter-digits and for different series lengths? Why was a digit series group matched with a letter-digit series group? Within each group the successive digits (or letters) were random with the constraint that no unit would be repeated in the next position, nor would they appear in logical sequence (like 1-2-3). Why was this done?

F. All the letter-digit series were arranged to produce pronounceable words. Remember that the telephone dial was used as the basis for translating a digit series to a letter-digit series. However, there are three letters assigned to each digit on the dial. What if we had chosen letters to form unpronounceable words. What would you predict the result would be?

G. If our limited short-term memory is the equivalent to having a computer with one bit of RAM instead of the usual megabytes, why isn't a computer a million times smarter than we are?

H. If long-term memory is not immutable, what implications does that have for aspects of society like the law, the licensing of professional practitioners, student examinations, and the recording of history?

Student _____ Section _____ Due Date _____

MEASURING SHORT-TERM MEMORY

1. Write an answer for question ___ from the Interpretation section of this project.

2. Write a formal Conclusions section for this experiment.

3. Include any material your instructor might require.

4. Attach Tables 8-1 and 8-2 and your graphs.

TABLE 8-1

FREQUENCY TABULATIONS OF CORRECT RECALLS

Subject No.	Memory Span Stimulus Type			
	Digits		Letter-Digits	
	Number Correct	Percent Correct	Number Correct	Percent Correct
1.				
2.				
3.				
4.				
5.				
6.				
7.				
8.				
9.				
10.				
11.				
12.				
13.				
14.				

Determine memory span as illustrated in the graph below.

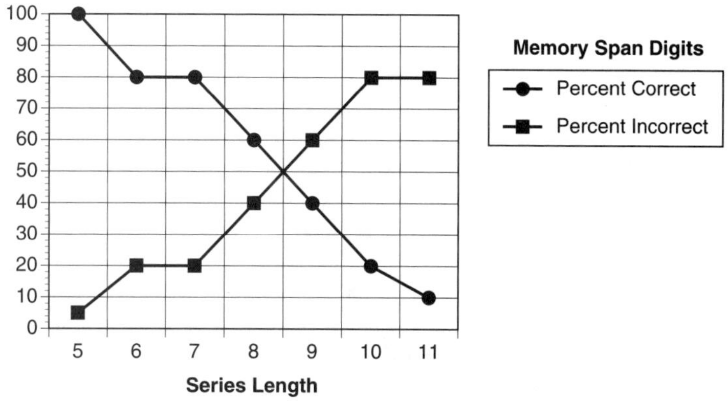

TABLE 8-2

SIGN TEST OF THE EFFECTS OF "CHUNKING" ON MEMORY SPAN

Subject No.	Memory Span — Letter Digits — Interpolated Score From Graph	Memory Span — Digits — Interpolated Score From Graph	Sign
1.			
2.			
3.			
4.			
5.			
6.			
7.			
8.			
9.			
10.			
11.			
12.			
13.			
14.			
15.			
16.			
17.			
18.			
19.			
20.			
	Significance Level ρ	Total No. of Plus Signs	

PROJECT 9

HOW FAST DO YOU THINK?

The concept of reaction time has proved useful to psychologists in a variety of practical situations ranging from basic research to clinical applications to measuring the speed of the brain's decision-making processes. For example, **simple reaction time** can be operationally defined as the time required by an individual to make a response signaling that he or she has seen or heard a stimulus. In simple reaction time, the specific stimulus and specific response are known to the subject. **Choice reaction time** is operationally defined as the time required to make a response when more than one stimulus is possible, each one requiring a particular response. In this case, the specific stimulus and response are not "automatic" but require a decision. Simple reaction time measures the time it takes the central nervous system to perceive a stimulus and make a motor response. Choice reaction time measures the time it takes the central nervous system to perceive a stimulus, make a decision about which stimulus and which response are required, and then make the motor response. At the risk of some oversimplification, you can estimate the time the brain requires to make such a decision by subtracting the average simple reaction time from the average choice reaction time.

Not only is reaction time a basic tool for the cognitive and neurosciences, it is also widely used in **industrial organizational psychology**. Human performance measurement has military, industrial, transportation, and auto safety applications where speed, precision, and errorless execution may be absolute requirements. How can we assess the limits? How much stress is tolerable and at what point is performance adversely affected?

1. Purposes

To determine an individual's average simple reaction time, average choice reaction time, and decision-making time. To correlate decision-making time with performance on the arcade game used in Project 5.

2. Apparatus

The Macintosh Reaction Time application and the experiment file Decision Time.

3. Procedure

Students are the subjects and collect simple and choice reaction time data using their preferred and nonpreferred hands for simple reaction time and for choice reaction time. The experiment uses a counterbalanced design to collect 10 simple reaction time measures (with 5 correct for each hand), then 20 choice reaction time measures (with 10 correct for each hand), and ends with 10 more simple reaction times. At the beginning of each section, there is an Information page so you know what to do. Table 9-1 can be filled in from your data window after you have completed the experiment. Look at it carefully as it shows which trials were test trials as opposed to Information pages and for which hand.

How Fast Do You Think?

An alternative to entering your data by hand is provided in the software. You can use the Decision Time Excel Macro in the Excel Data Templates folder to automatically score and plot your individual data. You will need to have available the spreadsheet application Excel.

Excel™ Data Templates

4. Data Analysis

Using Table 9-2, calculate your mean simple reaction time and choice reaction time for each hand. Determine the difference for your measure of decision time. In Table 9-3, you should have a record of your average score from Project 5.

Use Table 9-4 to test for the effect of simple vs. choice RT. Class data will be read out by subjects to complete the two left columns of Table 9-4. Similarly, use Table 9-5 to test the effect, if any, of hand preferences.

The purpose of Table 9-6 is to organize our data so that a correlation may be calculated. Use the mean decision time and mean arcade game score for both hands combined.

Correlation is the relation between two sets of data. A correlation coefficient is a descriptive statistic that measures the "going togetherness" of those two sets of data. Correlation does not show causality. For example, demographic data in the 1950s actually showed that when a high number of storks nested on the roofs in Holland, a higher number of babies were born. (We hope you are aware that storks don't *cause* babies.) This example illustrates a positive correlation, where high values of one variable (storks) go with high values of another variable (babies), and similarly low values with low values. The correlation statistic is arranged so that the maximum value of a positive correlation is +1.0. Note that the sign indicates the type of correlation (in this case positive) and the numerical value the measure of the degree of "going togetherness."

In a negative correlation, high values of one variable go together with low values of another. Again, correlation does not imply causality. For example, skill at typing, measured in words per minute, correlates negatively with foot size. That is, better typists have smaller feet! The maximum value of a negative correlation is -1.0. No relationship between two variables results in a correlation near 0.

For this project, we use the **Spearman rank-order correlation** to make a prediction. Depending on the sign and magnitude of our correlation, we might be able to answer the question of how well decision time predicts performance on an arcade game (or vice versa).

Prediction is one of the main uses of correlation. If you couldn't arrange a typing test, for example, but had to choose a typist, you could ask for the person's shoe size. The fact that this sounds silly in no way compromises your ability to make a good prediction. In fact, foot size is a better predictor even than are grades in high school typing courses. Foot size correlates about -.35 and grades about +.30. Since foot size is the larger correlation, it is, on the whole, the better *single* predictor of typing speed. Of course, by using both predictors together, we have an even greater chance of a successful selection. This concept is the basis of a technique called **regression analysis**. Use the following procedure to complete Table 9-6 and compute a correlation coefficient showing the relationship between decision time and arcade game performance.

Step 1. Separately rank the two columns of scores, with the fastest decision time and the highest arcade game scores each getting the rank of 1.

Step 2. Find the difference between the ranks for each subject and enter it in the column headed D (difference). If you have had ties in rank, some of your ranks will include the decimal .5, so be careful to carry the difference accurately into column D.

Step 3. Square the differences; that is, multiply the figure by itself, and enter the product in the next column, D^2 (difference squared). A very easy way to find the square of a difference that contains the decimal .5 is to multiply the whole number by the next higher whole number and add the fraction .25. Suppose one of your differences is 5.5. The square of 5.5 is 5 X 6 + .25 = 30.25.

Step 4. Add the squared differences and enter this total in the box for sum.

Step 5. Multiply the sum of the squared differences by six.

Step 6. Square the N; subtract 1, then multiply by N again.

Step 7. Divide the answer you got in step 6 into the answer you got in step 5.

Step 8. Subtract the answer you got in step 7 from 1.00. This gives you rho (ρ), the rank difference correlation coefficient. (Be careful that you handle minus signs correctly!)

Step 9. Use Table 9C to determine the level of significance. The statistical formula is a summary of a number of operations such as you have just performed. The formula for ρ is as follows:

The Spearman Rank-Order Correlation

$$\rho = 1 - \left(\frac{6 \Sigma D^2}{N(N^2 - 1)} \right)$$

D = difference in ranks

TABLE 9C

CRITICAL VALUES FOR SPEARMAN ρ

Sample Size (N) Number of Paired Scores	Significance level for the absolute value of ρ equal to or greater than the tabled value (Two-tailed test)	
	5% Level	1% Level
5	1.000	
6	.886	1.000
7	.786	.929
8	.715	.881
9	.700	.834
10	.649	.794
11	.619	.764
12	.588	.735
13	.561	.704
14	.539	.680
15	.522	.658
16	.503	.636
17	.488	.618
18	.474	.600
19	.460	.585
20	.447	.570
21	.437	.556
22	.426	.544
23	.417	.532
24	.407	.521
25	.398	.511

5. Interpretation

The following questions are for discussion, study, or review.

A. If you were to graph one variable on the abscissa and the other on the ordinate, how would a **scatter plot** of these data look? What would correlations of +1.0, 0, and -1.0 look like?

B. What degree of correlation would you expect to find between intelligence and scholastic success? Between IQ of parents and IQ of children? Between a good aptitude test and success on the job? In problems like these, psychologists have used correlation to advantage.

C. If the correlation between grades and hours spent in extracurricular activities were .52, what would you be willing to predict about a student's extracurricular participation if you knew only that his grade point average is 3.4?

D. What are the advantages and the limitations in correlation work?

E. Give three examples of reaction time that are important in everyday life.

F. Identify the independent variable, dependent variables, and controlled variables in this project.

G. The factor that causes a relationship between two correlated variables like storks and babies is called a **suppressor variable**. What could be the suppressor variable in this example? What might it be for foot size and secretarial ability?

H. Explain why foot size is a better predictor of typing speed than the grade in a typing course.

I. Is intelligence correlated with thinking quickly? Should society monitor mall video arcades to find potential applicants for starfighters, air traffic controllers, astronauts, and so forth?

J. What effect does age have on simple reaction time and on decision time?

K. Find a research article from a psychological journal where reaction time is one of the major dependent variables. Write a brief review or make a brief presentation to the class about what you have found.

Student _____ Section _____ Due Date _____

HOW FAST DO YOU THINK?

1. Write an answer for question ___ from the Interpretation section of this project.

2. Write a formal Conclusions section based on the results of this experiment. Refer to the IRP section for the correct form.

3. Include any additional material your instructor may require.

4. Attach Tables 9-1 through 9-6.

How Fast Do You Think?

TABLE 9-1

INDIVIDUAL SIMPLE AND CHOICE REACTION TIMES IN MILLISECONDS

Decision Time Raw Data					
Test Trial No.	Simple RT		Test Trial No.	Choice RT	
	Left	Right		Left	Right
2			14		
3			15		
4			16		
5			17		
6			18		
8			19		
9			20		
10			21		
11			22		
12			23		
35			24		
36			25		
37			26		
38			27		
39			28		
41			29		
42			30		
43			31		
44			32		
45			33		
$\overline{X} =$			$\overline{X} =$		
Preferred Hand:					

How Fast Do You Think?

TABLE 9-2

MEASURE OF REACTION TIME DECISION TIME

| Hand | Reaction Time ||| Decision Time |
	Choice RT	Simple RT	$\overline{X} =$	Choice RT − Simple RT
Left				
Right				
$\overline{X} =$				

TABLE 9-3

MEAN ARCADE GAME SCORE FROM PROJECT 5

Arcade Game:	
	Mean Score
Independent Variable Condition 1	
Independent Variable Condition 2	
Average Arcade Game Performance	

How Fast Do You Think?

TABLE 9-4

SIGN TEST: EFFECTS OF CHOICE VS. SIMPLE REACTION TIME

Subject No.	Reaction Time			Sign
	Choice RT Average Score From Table 9-2	Simple RT Average Score From Table 9-2	
1.			
2.			
3.			
4.			
5.			
6.			
7.			
8.			
9.			
10.			
11.			
12.			
13.			
14.			
15.			
16.			
17.			
18.			
19.			
20.			
Significance Level p		Total No. of Plus Signs	

How Fast Do You Think? 149

TABLE 9-5

SIGN TEST: EFFECTS OF HANDEDNESS ON REACTION TIME

Subject No.	Reaction Time — Preferred Hand — Average Score From Table 9-2	Reaction Time — Nonpreferred Hand — Average Score From Table 9-2	Sign
1.			
2.			
3.			
4.			
5.			
6.			
7.			
8.			
9.			
10.			
11.			
12.			
13.			
14.			
15.			
16.			
17.			
18.			
19.			
20.			
	Significance Level p	Total No. of Plus Signs	

TABLE 9-6

CORRELATION BETWEEN DECISION TIME AND GAME SCORE

Subject No.	Mean Scores (9-2 and 9-3) Decision Time	Mean Scores (9-2 and 9-3) Game Score	Ranks Decision Time	Ranks Game Score	D	D^2
1.						
2.						
3.						
4.						
5.						
6.						
7.						
8.						
9.						
10.						
11.						
12.						
13.						
14.						
15.						
16.						
17.						
18.						
19.						
20.						

$$\rho = 1 - \left(\frac{6 \Sigma D^2}{N(N^2 - 1)} \right)$$

Σ

$\rho =$

Significance Level ρ

PROJECT 10

ARE TWO HEADS BETTER THAN ONE?

Some superficial commentators have said that psychology is the study of the self-evident. But often with the self-evident, there can be two conflicting and apparently valid "truths." How, then, are we to choose between them? For example, the saying "two heads are better than one" is contradicted by the saying "too many cooks spoil the broth." Practical experience may tell us that each is true, or at least partly so. If we consider successful collaborations in business, science, or technology, we often discover that a "team effort" produces success. Conversely, we are suspicious of bureaucracies and probably know the joke with the punch line, "A camel is a horse designed by a committee."

Different areas of psychology such as **social psychology**, **industrial/organizational psychology**, and **cognitive psychology** each bring a unique disciplinary perspective. Social psychologists are interested in understanding the interactions between people and how they affect performance or behavior. The I/O psychologist is interested in overall business structure. For example, one business model might be an authoritarian administrative style, where one person is ultimately responsible for decisions. Another model might be a collaborative and distributed group decision-making style—a committee model, if you will. Cognitive psychologists are interested in thought processes, including strategies for solving problems. Like many things in psychology, no single view or single model for problem solving, business style, or cognitive strategy is correct; often the correct model depends on the circumstances. By studying such dependencies scientifically, psychology as a discipline has been able to resolve some of the complexities and apparent contradictions of more superficial approaches.

Psychologists often use games to study creativity and problem solving. You might use a game for a business simulation, as an example. What is the optimum group size for a particular type of problem? What personalities work best together? What role might gender play? Do not underestimate the value of games in establishing sound principles for both individuals and groups. You can train children and adults in various techniques to improve creativity and arrive at new and unique solutions. For example, you have probably heard of **brainstorming** as a group technique. Try to use some of its basic rules when you play the problem-solving game in your group for this project. The usual rules for brainstorming include an admonition to be tolerant of the suggestions of others, even when they apparently conflict with your own. Have the group generate as many ideas as possible. Have everyone attempt to be creative, think divergently, take risks, and change mental directions. Build on others' suggestions and, in later stages, try to bring order out of chaos.

1. Purposes

To investigate the influence of two variables—group size and the difficulty of the problem to be solved—on success in problem solving. To demonstrate the interaction of two independent variables.

2. Apparatus

The Problem Solving application and the experiment files Familiar Words and Unfamiliar Words.

3. Procedure

By setting up two different group sizes, one person or two, we can test the contradictory yet popular beliefs that "two heads are better than one" and "too many cooks spoil the broth."

Like many psychological phenomena, the results we get depend on the circumstances. In this project, we use a word game. Basically, the Macintosh program randomly selects a word from a file—in this case, either a familiar word or an unfamiliar word. Each is five letters long. By using astute guesses, combined with feedback from the program, your object is to discover the hidden word. Familiar words are **operationally defined** as coming from the 500 most used words in the Thorndike-Lorge list. Unfamiliar words are found less than 10 in one million times in popular writing. It may well turn out that our results depend on the particular values of each of the independent variables, group size and word familiarity. For example, for unfamiliar words, two heads might be "better than one," but the opposite might be true for familiar (easy) words.

Notice that we have two independent variables operating at the same time in this experiment. The advantage of this more than just saves time; it is the only way to discover the "that depends" sort of result often seen in social situations.

This concept of **interaction** deserves further explanation because it is a notion that has not been encountered before in our work. Suppose a friend asks you if you like science fiction movies. You might reply "that depends." Upon further questioning, you might explain that you enjoy that type of movie when "I'm in the mood." In brief, the type of movie you enjoy depends in part on the mood you are in. Therefore we say there is an interaction between movie type and your prevailing mood in determining the dependent variable, movie enjoyment. Whenever the reply "that depends" is appropriate, we might well suspect the possibility of an interaction. Thus, in an interaction, the effect of the level of one independent variable depends on the value of the levels of the other independent variable.

3.1 Rules for the Problem-Solving Task

All groups will follow these rules for solving each problem and determining the word the computer has selected. Each word is five letters in length. Proper names, abbreviations, foreign words, or four-letter words made plural or possessive by the addition of the letter *s* are not permitted. All words are standard English words. Because various restrictions have been placed on guesses in the application, following the rules is encouraged. Of course, you can circumvent them, but that's not the object!

The subject or subjects in the two-subject (2-S) group are given 45 seconds to enter a guess of the problem word. If no guess is made in that time, a guess is charged anyhow. The objective is to determine the problem word in the smallest possible number of guesses. The software keeps track of timing.

After each guess is made, the computer indicates how many "hits" of individual letters are contained in the guess. A hit is a letter identical to one in the hidden word and in exactly the same position. For example, if the problem word is "black" and the subject guesses "plank," he or she has made three hits. The software should be set so that it does not tell which letters are direct hits, only how many. Notice that the software can give varying levels and types of feedback. Interestingly enough, scores are often better when only the "number of correct letters in correct position" feedback is given, as in our experiment. More feedback, like having the "number of correct letters in wrong position" disrupts problem solving. If you are familiar with the game Mastermind, you should recognize this latter case and perhaps see a possible IRP study.

In the 1-S groups, the problem must be solved by the subject alone, but there is no constraint on how subjects in the 2-S group operate. However, the procedure of taking turns at guessing is not desirable. Try instead to follow some of the principles of brainstorming.

Depending on time available, you might make a more elegant experiment by running at least two problems of each level of familiarity in counterbalanced order. Depending on the number of students in your class, you may need to combine data with another section in order to do a statistical analysis.

4. Descriptive Analysis of Results

Data must be secured for the entire class and entered in Tables 10-1 and 10-2. Take care to avoid incorrect entries. Class data will be in terms of the total number of guesses required to solve each type of problem for each team.

Are Two Heads Better Than One?

Make a graph of your results by plotting the means. Table 10-3 illustrates a sample graph. The ordinate scale is the mean number of guesses required; the abscissa has just two points: 1-S and 2-S groups. Plot one curve for familiar stimuli and another for unfamiliar stimuli on the same graph. The more the two curves differ in slope or tilt, the more likely that you have an interaction. Your instructor will help you interpret the interaction in this graph.

5. STATISTICAL ANALYSIS OF RESULTS

Recall that we are, in a sense, running two experiments simultaneously: the effect of group size and the effect of stimulus type. Furthermore, each observation (or datum) is obtained on a group. Now, since each group solved both familiar and unfamiliar word problems, these scores are not independent. Therefore, we should test the significance of this difference with the sign test, ignoring for the moment the variable of group size.

However, groups are independent of each other. We have no basis for comparing any particular 1-S group with any particular 2-S group. It is, therefore, proper to use the *U*-test to analyze the possible effect of group size. The procedure for analysis is still basically to have only one variable changing at a time in an experiment. Thus, in effect, we hold one of the independent variables constant over all conditions while the other independent variable is observed. For example, in looking at the main effect of group size, we include both familiar and unfamiliar word data so that the effects of word familiarity are the same for both size groups.

Each of these procedures can help answer the two separate questions in the project, but they will not tell us if there is significant interaction. Your instructor may have time to describe how such a test, like an **analysis of variance (ANOVA)**, is made, but the actual computation will not be attempted in class.

6. INTERPRETATION

The following questions are for discussion, study and review.

A. Define the following terms: problem solving, interaction, 2 X 2 experimental design, operational definition, ANOVA, cognitive psychology.

B. What are the hypotheses of this study? Identify the independent variables, the dependent variables, and controlled variables.

C. Describe how you developed strategies of problem solving in your group. Did these strategies develop differently in 1-S groups than they did in 2-S groups?

D. Explain in your own words why it was proper to use the sign test for one of our two problems and the U-test for the other.

E. Can you recall any practical problem you encountered that resembled in any way either the strategies you developed as a problem solver in this project or the findings about the experimental variables?

F. What generalizations might you make to other group processes—for example to business or politics?

G. What factors have psychologists identified that promote creative thinking.

H. Identify the main impediments we sometimes face in effective problem solving. Give a real-life example from your own experience that illustrates one of these impediments.

I. Identify and briefly explain some of the rules or approaches for successful problem solving, including heuristics, analogies, algorithms, changing mental set, and parceling subgoals.

Student _____ Section _____ Due Date _____

ARE TWO HEADS BETTER THAN ONE?

1. Write an answer for question ___ from the Interpretation section of this project.

2. Write an abstract of an experiment you might design to test for the effects of the amount of information feedback on problem solving. Try and make it suitable as a proposal for the Individual Research Project.

Are Two Heads Better Than One?

3. Briefly state the results obtained from this experiment.

4. Include any additional material your instructor may require.

5. Attach Tables 10-1, 10-2, and 10-3 and your graph.

TABLE 10-1

MAIN EFFECT OF WORD FAMILIARITY ON THE PROBLEM-SOLVING TASK

Subject No.	Familiar Words	Unfamiliar Words	Sign
	\multicolumn{2}{c	}{Number of Guesses by 1-S Group}	
1.			
2.			
3.			
4.			
5.			
6.			
7.			
8.			
9.			
10.			
	Significance Level ρ	Total No. of Plus Signs	
	\multicolumn{2}{c	}{Number of Guesses by 2-S Group}	
1.			
2.			
3.			
4.			
5.			
6.			
7.			
8.			
9.			
10.			
	Significance Level ρ	Total No. of Plus Signs	

TABLE 10-2

MAIN EFFECT OF GROUP SIZE ON THE PROBLEM-SOLVING TASK

Group Size in Problem Solving			
Combined Rank	Score	Ranks 1-S	Ranks 2-S
1			
2			
3			
4			
5			
6			
7			
8			
9			
10			
11			
12			
13			
14			
15			
16			
17			
18			
19			
20			
Σ			
Significance Level	p		

Combine the scores from both groups of data and list them in rank order in the Score column.

If the score came from the group in the "light gray" Ranks column, enter its rank in that column.

If the score came from the group in the "medium gray" Ranks column, enter its rank in that column.

If scores are tied, assign an average rank to the appropriate columns.

Sum the two Ranks columns. subtract the LARGEST sum from the constant determined by group size in Table B of the Appendix and determine the significance level.

TABLE 10-3

SUMMARY OF WORD FAMILIARITY X GROUP SIZE INTERACTION

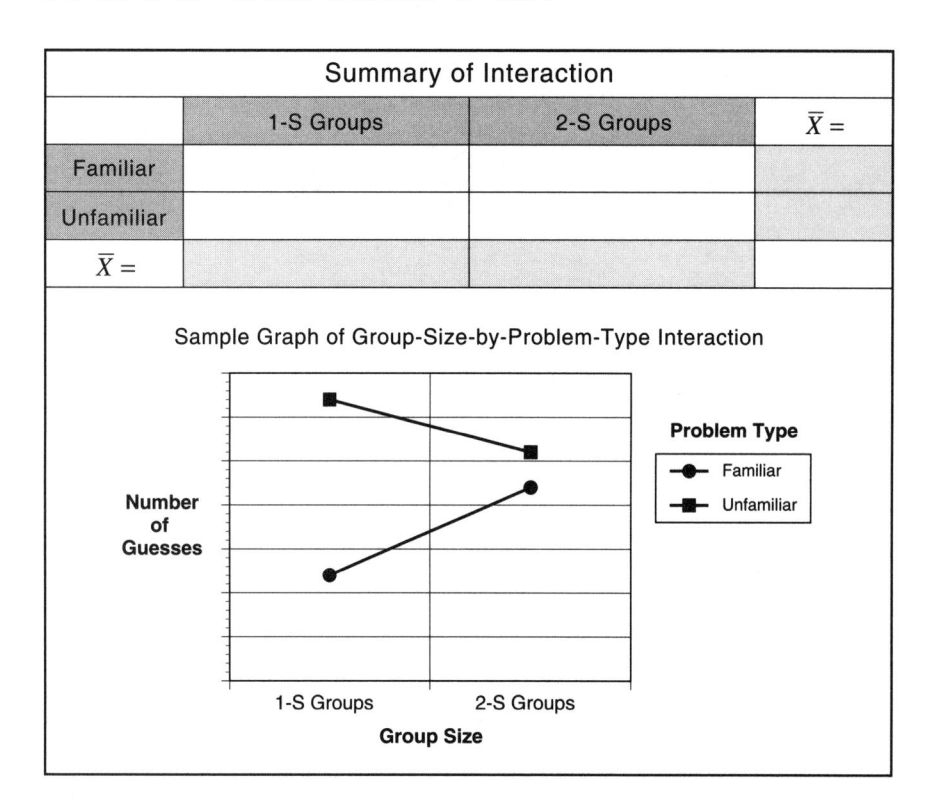

Summary of Interaction				
	1-S Groups	2-S Groups	$\bar{X} =$
Familiar			
Unfamiliar			
$\bar{X} =$			

Sample Graph of Group-Size-by-Problem-Type Interaction

Number of Guesses

Group Size: 1-S Groups, 2-S Groups

Problem Type:
- ● Familiar
- ■ Unfamiliar

PROJECT 11

MANIPULATING MENTAL IMAGES

Thinking can involve language or mental images or both. People seem to differ in their preferences for, and use of, these different thinking strategies. Imagine your mother with a beard. Do you see a mental image? Does language play a role in your thoughts? Imagine the route you took to get from where you live to class. Do you have a **cognitive map** of the route? How would you provide explicit directions to a visitor? Interestingly, our cognitive maps often contain systematic distortions of the "real" world. We tend to oversimplify and have a rectilinear two-dimensional bias. Do you recall in the *Star Trek* movie *The Wrath of Khan* the battle scene in the nebula where Kirk defeats Khan because of the latter's inexperienced bias for two-dimensional tactics?

As a research technique, reaction time has been used to discover how our brains handle and process mental images. For example, do we scan a mental image as if we were looking at a "photograph"? Researchers seem to think so. A subject might be shown a picture, such as the astronaut on page 172. Before reading on, turn the page and study the picture for a minute starting with the face plate; try to retain a complete mental image when you turn back and continue reading. Make sure you study the picture, starting with the astronaut's face and moving outward.

In an experiment, the picture is then hidden and the subject is asked questions about the mental image of the astronaut he or she retains in memory. Again, start with your mental image at the astronaut's face. If you were asked this question, you should have a short reaction time: Can you see the reflections in the face plate? The next two questions would yield an intermediate reaction time, presumably because it would take longer to scan your mental image to get the answer: Does he wear a flag on his sleeve? Are both hands on the controls for the jet pack? The longest reaction times would be prompted by this question: Is one of his shoe laces untied? Did you scan your mental image to answer those questions? If subjects scan their mental images, their reaction time to the first question will be shorter than their reaction time to the last question. Can you create a similar experiment for your IRP? What controls are necessary?

Another type of experiment on mental imagery involves our ability to manipulate images, for example by rotation. Subjects are shown a three-dimensional drawing or picture in one orientation and a second drawing rotated to a different orientation. To determine if the drawings are identical, the subject must rotate his or her own mental image to determine a match. The further the rotation required, the longer the reaction time. Thus, our processing of mental images seems similar to the types of manipulations we would perform on the real objects themselves. Might this explain how and why we use our hands when describing certain thoughts or ideas?

In your library look up one of the first experiments concerning mental rotation. The citation is:

Sheppard, R. & Metzler, J. (1971). Mental rotation of three dimensional objects. *Science, 171,* 701–703.

Another idea for an IRP project is to experiment with the observation that we often have a standard representational format for familiar objects in our mental images. For example, the picture of the astronaut naturally seems the "right way up." But this standard view may make it more difficult for us to perceive other information that may in fact be true. Is the North Pole above the horizon at the top of the picture? If you were from South America, South Africa, Australia, or New Zealand and maybe less "anti" antipodes, would it be easier to see that the South Pole is up? If you turn your laboratory manual upside down, does this help you see it as the South Pole? Which is really true? Can you tell by the sun's reflection?

In this project we do a mental imagery experiment similar to the "three mountain task" of developmental psychologist Jean Piaget. In that experiment, a child was seated at a table on which

Manipulating Mental Images

were arranged three different mountains. The child was then asked to imagine the scene from the viewpoint of a doll seated at different locations around the table. Children younger than about eight years of age, in the **preoperational stage** of development, usually cannot take a "different point of view." They are quite **egocentric** and report that their own view must be the view of the doll.

In our experiment you will be shown an arrangement of objects from a toy train set. The next view will be of the same objects rotated left or right to varying degrees, up to 180. You need to determine if the angle of view has moved to the left or to the right by entering Left or Right, as appropriate. Subjects also respond Yes or No to the question: Are the objects in the same relative position to one another or is this a mirror image? Thus, if the objects are simply rotated left and are in the same position, the answer would be entered as Left-Yes. For some trials the objects will be rotated, say again to the Left, but rearranged as a mirror image. This is an impossible actual rotation and therefore would be answered Left-No. Reaction Time measurements to the correct response will be recorded. This task is very difficult and requires concentration. To help, there is a practice trial or two. We might hypothesize that the greater the rotation in the second view, the longer the Reaction Time, presumably because it takes longer for the subject to mentally rotate the image. We might also hypothesize that "No" trials, where the objects have been rearranged, have slower RTs.

1. PURPOSES

To measure Reaction Time for varying degrees of mental rotation of a stimulus arrangement. To use a graphical approach to viewing different hypotheses that may be extracted from the **Raw Data**.

2. APPARATUS

A Macintosh with the application Reaction Time and the experiment file Mental Rotation. If your Macintosh has sufficient memory, make sure the Reaction Time application's memory size is about 2000K, and run the color version of Mental Rotation from the *MacLaboratory* CD. The spreadsheet and graphing application Excel is convenient to have since an automatic data analysis macro is included with the software.

Section 3 Cognitive Sciences

3. Procedure

The file Mental Rotation contains a set of instructions for subjects, some initial practice trials, and then the experiment itself.

3.1 Instructions

The instructions are designed to ensure that the subject understands the task.

3.2 Practice Trials

The practice trials serve two purposes: (1) to familiarize the subject with the experiment and (2) to provide for **warm-up** to responding. The practice trials also tend to reduce within-subject random variability, which is desirable because practical limitations of time allow us to have only one trial for each rotation angle that is a Yes response and a similar one for each No response.

3.3 Experiment Trials

The experiment consists of randomly mixed trials, where an initial stimulus arrangement is presented followed by a simple rotation about the y-axis of the same relative arrangement (Yes response) or a mirror image relative arrangement (No response). The apparent angles of rotation are 45°, 90°, 135°, and 180° to the left, and similarly to the right.

4. Data Analysis

After conducting the experiment, save your data as both a text file and an experiment file. The data contain a Correct Responses Code so you can identify which reaction time is associated with which type and degree of rotation. Table 11-1 shows the code contained in the Correct Responses column of your electronic data field.

4.1 Individual Raw Data

Open your data and transcribe the relevant entries into Table 11-1 for yourself as a subject.

4.2 Group Raw Data

To fill out Table 11-2, the class must transcribe each person's individual raw data, being careful to keep a consistent order. You might also indicate the sex of each subject because you might want to consider whether the sex of the subject affects ability to perform mental image rotations.

4.3 Graphic Analysis

In this project we do not do any statistical tests although you certainly could for some hypotheses. Rather, we use the spreadsheet and graphing application to present the raw data in ways that will most clearly illustrate various hypotheses. For example, the sample graph of individual data in Table 11-1 is arranged to easily compare the Yes vs. No response conditions for that subject. Your first graph, for your individual data, will be similar. Your next task is to design clear graphic presentations to illustrate each of the hypotheses in section 4.4 below using the group data. (You may be able to illustrate more than one hypothesis with the same graph.) Because of the possibility of **eccentric variance** due to the small number of trials, it may be best to use **medians** and not means where possible.

4.4 Hypotheses

These hypotheses are stated as general questions. You should restate them in a more formal way in the caption for each of your graphs.

- Do Yes response rotations have faster RTs than No response rotations?
- Is the speed of mental rotation a constant?
- Is there a preference for left- or right-hand rotation?
- Are there observable differences due to sex?
- Is a 180-degree rotation easier than lesser degrees of rotation?
- Are rectilinear rotations (90 or 180 degrees) easier than diagonal rotations (45 or 135 degrees)?
- If you consider the order of presentation from your electronic data, is there evidence for **progressive error**?
- Is the **variability** consistent across conditions?

Manipulating Mental Images

5. Interpretation

The following questions are for discussion, study, and review.

A. Identify the following terms: mental rotation, preoperational stage, eccentric variance, warm-up, egocentric, standard representation.

B. What effect might neuropsychological conditions like hemispheric laterality or specific learning disabilities have on mental rotation?

C. What is the relationship between ability at mental rotation and other mental imagery like dreaming?

D. Provide examples of applications to engineering psychology or human factors research.

E. What is the "three mountain task"? When do moral judgments become less egocentric in the course of normal human development?

Student _____ Section _____ Due Date _____

MANIPULATING MENTAL IMAGES

1. Attach your tables and graphs. Make sure each graph has a caption stating how it illustrates an hypothesis from the project.

TABLE 11-1

INDIVIDUAL RAW DATA FOR MENTAL IMAGE ROTATION

Correct Responses Code	Your RT Score (Correct)	Experimental Condition
y&r&1		Yes, same arrangement, Rotated right, 45 degrees
y&r&2		Yes, same arrangement, Rotated right, 90 degrees
y&r&3		Yes, same arrangement, Rotated right, 135 degrees
y&l&1		Yes, same arrangement, Rotated left, 45 degrees
y&l&2		Yes, same arrangement, Rotated left, 90 degrees
y&l&3		Yes, same arrangement, Rotated left, 135 degrees
y&4		Yes, same arrangement, Rotated 180 degrees
n&r&1		No, different arrangement, Rotated right, 45 degrees
n&r&2		No, different arrangement, Rotated right, 90 degrees
n&r&3		No, different arrangement, Rotated right, 135 degrees
n&l&1		No, different arrangement, Rotated left, 45 degrees
n&l&2		No, different arrangement, Rotated left, 90 degrees
n&l&3		No, different arrangement, Rotated left, 135 degrees
n&4		No, different arrangement, Rotated 180 degrees

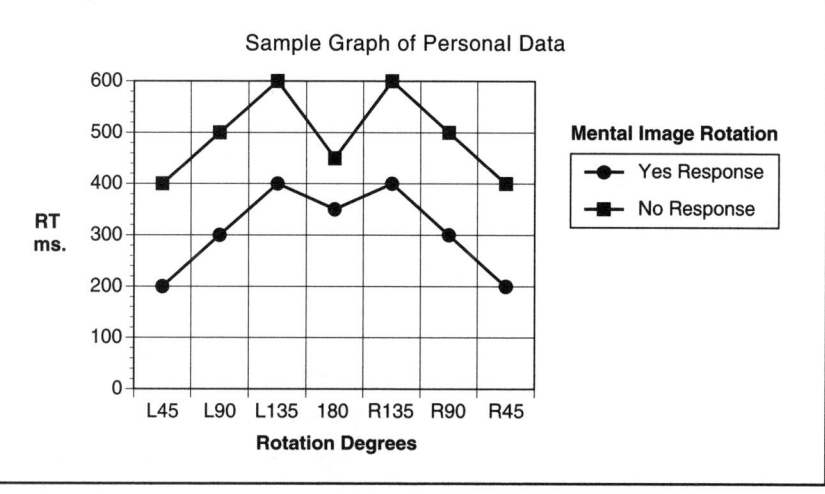

Sample Graph of Personal Data

Mental Image Rotation
- ● Yes Response
- ■ No Response

RT ms. vs. Rotation Degrees (L45, L90, L135, 180, R135, R90, R45)

TABLE 11-2

GROUP RAW DATA FOR MENTAL IMAGE ROTATION

Subject No.	yr1	yr2	yr3	y13 1	y13 2	y13 3	y 4	nr1	nr2	nr3	n13 1	n13 2	n13 3	n 4	MDN
1.															
2.															
3.															
4.															
5.															
6.															
7.															
8.															
9.															
10.															
11.															
12.															
13.															
14.															
15.															
16.															
17.															
18.															
19.															
20.															
MDN															

PROJECT 12

NEURAL MODELING IN VISUAL PERCEPTION

An important part of science (sometimes neglected in science education) is the development of theories and models. We often think of such theory building as the prerogative of senior scientists; yet, the history of science and technology often shows that major theoretical developments are made by young investigators just embarking on their careers. This project on neural modeling in visual perception is loosely based on the work of Nobel laure-

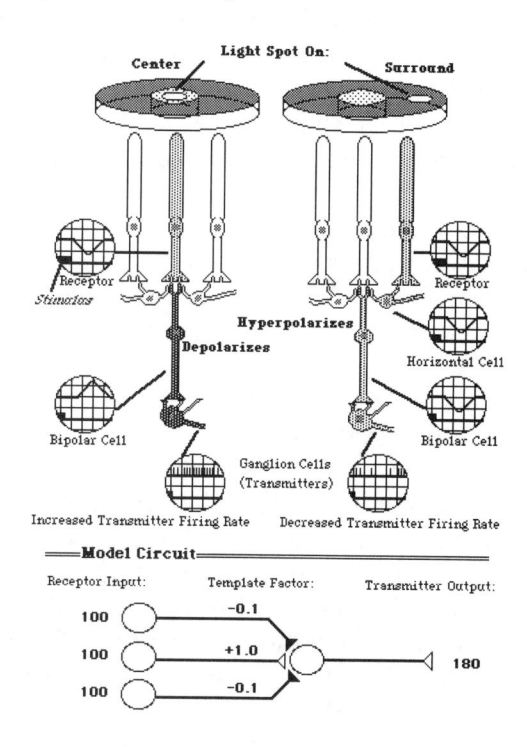

183

ates David Hubel and Thorsten Wiesel as developed for the Macintosh environment by my colleague Professor Tom Hewett (1985).

The text files on the disk can be opened with most word processors; they provide a detailed background for the model systems and organize a set of progressively more difficult exercises. Fundamentally, for this project you will design some model neural networks to solve two unknown visual system circuits showing **simultaneous contrast** and construct model circuits illustrating **lateral inhibition** and **motion detectors**. The data source for the model networks you construct comes from the area of **physiological psychology**. Researchers in this field and other basic neuroscientists pioneered the techniques for microelectrode recordings of the activity of neurons.

In the visual fields we are modeling, a microelectrode is inserted into a portion of the retina, and the activity that results from the presentation of various stimuli is observed. The spreadsheets allow you to record, with your theoretical microelectrode, the activity of visual receptor cells (e.g., **rod receptors**) and transmitter cells (e.g., **ganglion cells**). Ganglion cells have a resting rate of neural discharge that is 100 "spikes" per minute for our examples. Stimulation of a receptor either increases (**excitation**) or decreases (**inhibition**) the firing rate of the ganglion cell.

The illustration on the previous page shows, in schematic form, the arrangement of receptors, **horizontal cells**, **bipolar cells**, and ganglion cells, of the vertebrate retina. Horizontal cells and bipolar cells do not have **action potentials** per se, rather depolarization increases and hyperpolarization decreases the amount of **neurotransmitter** released. Our representation of a **receptive field** has been simplified for the purposes of this project. When constructing your own neural circuits, use the convention in the model circuit illustrated to show inhibitory and excitatory effects. Perhaps the most important feature of receptive fields is that they respond to different shapes or line orientations of different angles or lengths. The models you create for simultaneous contrasts relate to the observation that one type of receptive field consists roughly of a circular center in the middle of a larger circular surround. A spot of light to the center increases the firing rate of the transmitter cell. Light in the surround decreases the firing rate. (Incidentally, when a light to the surround is turned off, trans-

Neural Modeling in Visual Perception

mitter cell firing rate briefly shows an increased burst of firing.) In other types of receptive fields, the response to light is reversed between center and surround. In creating circuits for lateral inhibition and motion detection, you need to consider a number of receptive fields and their transmitter cell output as well as their interactions.

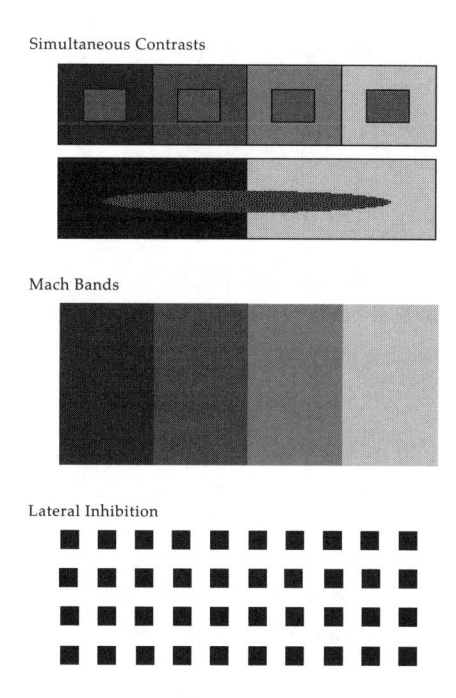

Simultaneous Contrasts

Mach Bands

Lateral Inhibition

Our straightforward spreadsheet-based systems do an adequate job at modeling perceptual phenomena such as simultaneous contrasts, Mach bands, and lateral inhibition. In the Mach bands illustrated above, note that the gray rectangles are not uniform in brightness. What utility does this have for visual systems?

1. Purpose

To create model neural networks illustrating perceptual phenomena in vision.

2. Apparatus

Macintosh, a spreadsheet application such as Excel, and the templates supplied with *MacLaboratory for Psychology* software.

Neural Modeling

3. Procedures

Consult the two references listed for operating instructions and numerous clues to help you decipher how to satisfy the requirements of this project.

4. Neural Models

Construct neural models for the two unknowns, lateral inhibition and motion detection, as described in the text files.

5. Interpretation

The following questions are for discussion, study, and review.

A. Define: lateral inhibition, simultaneous contrast, rod, cone, bipolar cell, amocrine cell, horizontal cell, ganglion cell, fovea centralis, synapse, hyperpolarization, depolarization, and neurotransmitter.

B. Outline the path of visual input from receptor to cortex.

C. Distinguish between sensation and perception.

D. What are **successive contrasts**? What neurophysiological processes might be involved in the phenomenon of **after-images**?

E. What neural processes are involved in the "rebound" of activity seen when stimulation to the surround is removed in center-on receptive fields?

F. How could knowledge of simultaneous contrasts affect engineering design?

6. References

Hewett, T.T. (1985) Teaching students to model neural circuits and neural networks using an electronic spreadsheet simulator. *Behavior Research Methods, Instruments & Computers, 17* (2), 339–344.

Hewett, T.T. (1986) Using an electronic spreadsheet simulator to teach neural modeling of visual phenomena. *Collegiate Microcomputers, 4* (2), 141–151.

Student _____ Section _____ Due Date _____

NEURAL MODELING IN VISUAL PERCEPTION

1. Briefly summarize the work for which Hubel and Wiesel were awarded the Nobel Prize. You might consult:

   Hubel, D. H., & Wiesel, T. N. (1979) Brain mechanisms of vision. *Scientific American, 241,* 150–162.

2. Attach your schematic drawings of the neural circuits required by your instructor. You may also be asked to hand in your own spreadsheet models.

INTRODUCTION

SECTION 4
LEARNING AND CONDITIONING

The wonder about learning is that it happens at all. What permanently changes in a cell or a brain in even a single learning trial? Learning occurs in even the most primitive organisms; that is, some event or stimulus occurs in the environment that leads to a long-lasting change in behavior or thought. The thing that makes learning so interesting to psychologists is that, on the one hand, it seems so difficult and, on the other, it seems all too easy and automatic. Consider learning a foreign language, or calculus, or memorizing a poem—these all seem difficult for most people and require focused **attention**, **motivation**, and effort. Consider learning to smoke cigarettes, or gambling with slot machines, or becoming afraid of airplanes, or learning the love of money—these all seem easy to acquire. Paradoxically, if it seems easy to learn, it often seems very hard to "unlearn," as anyone with an addiction or a **phobia** may readily attest. It is important to understand basic principles of learning so that, at least, you will know how essential it is to set a good example for youngsters. Understanding principles of learning will also help you be a more knowledgeable consumer. It will also help you answer certain questions: Why doesn't sleep learning work? Why are claims that we don't use 80% of our brains untrue? Psychologists generally use three approaches to study learning: **operant conditioning, classical conditioning**, and **cognitive learning**.

In operant conditioning, a behavior carried out by an organism may be reinforced. If it is, it is more likely to occur again. We have all had the experience of earning a "gold star" and been motivated to continue along the same successful path. Money seems to be a very positive **reinforcement**; it increases the probability of continuing behaviors, like work, that tend to provide it! How do gold stars and money become reinforcing? If the frequency or timing of reinforcements is manipulated, it produces quite dramatic effects on behavior. Consider the slot machines common in casinos. They deliver change at a variable rate, relatively infrequently. We would say they deliver a reinforcement on a **variable-rate schedule**. This schedule of **partial reinforcement** yields a very high **rate of responding**—that is, putting in money and pulling the lever—and a high resistance to **extinction**—that is, continuing to do it for a long time in the absence of reinforcement. Are we like rats in a Skinner box or puppets on a string? Is this how "brainwashing" is managed? *MacLaboratory* provides

Introduction

two means of investigating operant conditioning principles. In one, you may actually be using real rats in operant chambers. *Controller* allows you to set up and program for yourself various conditioning contingencies. It also can be used as a logic trainer in scheduling or it can process control of anything, not just Skinner boxes. This is typically the approach in more advanced courses, often with majors, where the expense and ethical concerns about appropriate use of animals in research are more easily met. The second means of investigating operant conditioning principles is to use the simulation Sniffy, the virtual rat. Here you can experiment with **shaping** and conditioning different behaviors—for example, scratching or bar pressing. Sniffy also lets you test different schedules of reinforcement.

In classical conditioning, a previously neutral stimulus is associated or paired with a naturally meaningful stimulus. With pairing, the neutral stimulus becomes a predictor of events and itself becomes meaningful and capable of eliciting responses. The most famous example concerns Pavlov's dog, where a bell paired with food eventually came to elicit salivation all by itself. Most psychologists believe that pairing certain stimuli like insects, or airplanes, or elevators, with strong emotions is one cause of phobia development. Do advertisers intentionally pair their product names with other emotions—for example with emotions that might be elicited by viewing enticing women or cute babies? Normally we think the best conditioning occurs when the advertiser's name precedes and overlaps with the emotion-eliciting stimuli. Try keeping a notebook record of a sample of commercials. Are the stimuli arranged in a way that promotes classical conditioning? Can you make QuickTime movies on your Macintosh and use them with the application Reaction Time to investigate the best possible arrangement of advertising materials? Or, if your Macintosh isn't powerful enough, can you nevertheless set up an experiment to pair a stimulus, suppose the color red, with placing lemon crystals on the tongue? Will people be like Pavlov's dog? If you know you are going to be conditioned, can you prevent it by concentration or some other thought process? How might conditioning regarding food affect such disorders as **anorexia** and **bulimia**? Before actually designing an experiment in classical conditioning, you may want to thoroughly investigate the simulation called *Polygraph* in your software. This simulation is of the classical conditioning of emotion. You can study the arousal value of words, and pair stimuli in various ways to learn the effects of various pairing contingencies.

Cognitive learning recognizes that a good deal of human and higher animal behavior comes from modeling or copying the behavior of others or from observing the environment. Rats, for example, will develop a **cognitive map** of their surroundings, as will people for that matter, in the apparent absence of any reinforcement. Children may acquire habits and attitudes by simply observing the habits and attitudes of the various role models surrounding them. In learning the richness and complexity of our native languages, dialect, accent, and other language components are apparently primarily acquired through modeling. One distinguishing feature of the cognitive approach is that learning may occur in the absence of observable behavior. If you consider the implications of cognitive mapping, you might be able to generate some interesting hypotheses for an IRP report. If males have a supposed advantage in spatial relationships, do they have more accurate or more elaborate cognitive maps? If females have a superiority for language, is that because they are better at modeling language patterns? Might you then expect that they could memorize poems better or learn lyrics to songs more quickly? What role does modeling play in fads or in high school cliques? Suppose you got a couple of the popular trend setters on campus or in your high school to start a new fad. How long would it take to spread? Who picks it up first?

PROJECT 13

OPERANT CONDITIONING OF THE RAT

An unfortunate consequence of the difficulty and expense of running an operant conditioning laboratory is that students get little or no practical experience with the basic techniques and procedures. However, if you end up in psychology, or medicine, or an allied health profession, or education, or social work, or criminal justice, or government, or veterinary medicine, or biology, or even business, you may well use operant conditioning techniques in your day-to-day work. For example, operant conditioning is the basis of **biofeedback**, behavior management, and business motivation programs.

To achieve a fundamental understanding of concepts, you need to deal with them and handle them, not as an abstract exercise, but as the core techniques to achieving your specific goal. With this laboratory, you will get immediate feedback on the decisions you make. If you become frustrated or irritated, your situation will probably get worse. If you have studied and planned ahead, things will probably go quite well. As you work through this project learn the concepts and definitions that are presented at each stage. The more you are able to experiment directly with them, the easier it will be for you to consolidate and organize your accumulating knowledge and experience with operant conditioning techniques.

To provide some structure and limits to both you and the rat you will condition, the rat will work in a **Skinner box** for a food reinforcement. You must keep careful laboratory records and look after your rat carefully, as instructed.

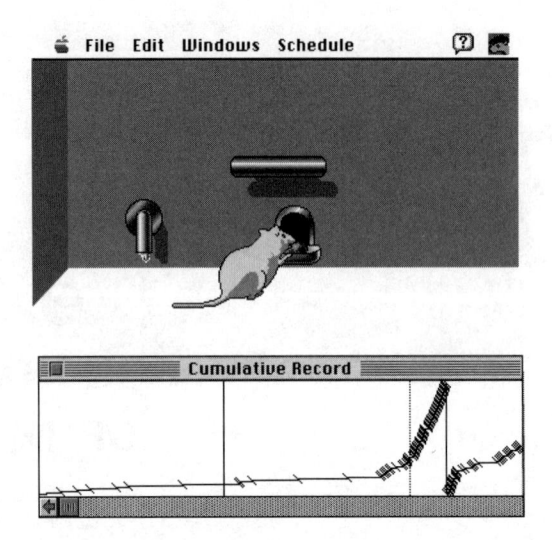

Methodologically, operant conditioning is a bit different from other experimental designs. It focuses on the individual organism being trained. Thus, if the organism did not engage in a behavior before shaping and conditioning, but does later, then you don't need a large sample or statistics to claim an effect. This approach is sometimes called an "*n*-of-one" study, or a case study. An essential beginning in any operant study is to measure **operant level** in order to establish a base line.

1. PURPOSE

To establish the conditioned bar press response in the rat.

2. APPARATUS

Skinner box and food reinforcements. Some of you may be using the application called *Controller*, which serves as a Boolean-type toolkit; this software allows Macintosh to automate and run the apparatus.

Alternatively, you may conduct a large part of this project with Sniffy, the virtual rat. This lifelike simulation was developed by Dr. Tom Alloway, Dr. Lester Krames, and Dr. Jeff Graham of the University of Toronto's Department of Psychology. Their intention was to provide a realistic conditioning experience in a cost-effective and ethical way. Sniffy exhibits some 15 different behaviors, any one of which can be shaped and conditioned. To make your experience as close to the actual as possible, we use the same

Operant Conditioning of the Rat

instructions with Sniffy as with a live rat. In places where the Sniffy icon appears, as it does here, you will find special notes.

3. Procedure

This project requires more than one laboratory period, and its success depends heavily on your preparation and skill in following the instruction provided. You should approach the task in terms of successive steps of more complex communication with your subject, keeping in mind that rats have limited visual perceptual capability.

Above all, you need to be patient and very quiet at all times. Avoid sudden movements, talking loudly, laughing, chair scraping, and all the other distractions that we ignore, but that can be traumatic to the rat. Keep the laboratory clean. Perhaps most important for success is to make "friends" with your rat. If you allow 20 minutes for the rat to crawl around unrestricted in the crook of your arm or the palm of your hand, you will find the remainder of the experiment pleasant and enjoyable (and so will the rat). Your instructor will allow time for you to become friendly with **Rattus norwegicus** while he or she explains the operation of the equipment to others in your group.

You may progress through the various stages of more and more complex learning described below as far as your time and skill permit, but every rat should be taken at least through step F, and some members of the class should be able to show the effects of **partial reinforcement** by working with a schedule of reinforcement as outlined in step I. To prepare for each step, ensure that your equipment is operating properly, that you have planned ahead, and that you are prepared to record data. For step A, do not operate the food (or water) reinforcement delivery mechanism or press the bar yourself. If you are working near a window, be sure the blinds are closed to avoid excessive distraction.

Students will work in teams of two or three experimenters to each rat as directed. You should have a firm agreement on the role of each person at the start and stick to the job you have agreed to do. One should operate the apparatus, another should accept responsibility for recording data (although all will eventually need a copy), and the third experimenter should handle the rat. Charts for the manual recording of data are included. If you are using software, note that the software keeps only limited data, such as bar presses, and it might be wise to keep your own independent records. Keep in mind at all times that your objective is to isolate one bit of behavior in the rat's repertoire (bar pressing) and to increase the probability of its occurrence (rate) by the method of reinforcement.

Step A. Observation

Place the rat gently in the box and quietly close the lid. Observe its behavior for five minutes, making notes in Table 13-1 on everything it does minute by minute. Every experimenter should do this in step A to increase the completeness of the report. Be very specific and objective in your observations—for example, "washes genitals," "stands on hind legs," "sticks nose into corner," "scratches left side," and so forth. Avoid vague notations and do not report in terms of what you think he may be "thinking about." At the bottom of the table, summarize your observations by indicating the number of different behaviors noted, the four most frequent, and the number of times each occurred. For this summary, consult the notes of the others in your group for behaviors you might have missed.

Step B. Operant Level of the Bar Press Response

Immediately after step A, begin a 10-minute observation of the operant, or base, level of the response we are going to condition. We are checking that the rat is capable of making the desired response. We would have considerable difficulty increasing the probability of a response unless the rat was capable of making it. For this observation, record in Table 13-2 (using slash marks: ///// /////, and so on) every time the rat touches the bar with its paw, and in a separate column, every time it presses the bar. A press is arbitrarily defined as one that produces a click in the apparatus. The software will save cumulative data of the bar presses, or you may keep them manually on graph paper as you go along. Either way, you will have an up-to-the-minute record of the responses "so far."

STEP C. MAGAZINE TRAINING

The objective in step C is to train the animal to go to a particular place (the water dipper or magazine) for its reinforcements. Your patience and skill become increasingly important from this point on. Deliver one reinforcement at a time when the rat is relatively inactive. The click and the sound of the reinforcement delivery may disrupt the rat and cause it to take a while to find the reinforcement. Be patient and very quiet. After the rat has consumed the reinforcement but not moved too far from the magazine, deliver another. Continue this training by delivering one reinforcement at a time and waiting until the rat consumes it and moves away before delivering the next one. Success at this stage requires a clean magazine. It should be washed out before the start of every session. This training is critical for the success of later steps. You are trying to "tell" the rat that it has a reinforcement when it hears a click and to train it to find the reinforcement. You need to continue this training until magazine approach behavior is well established. Usually no more than 15 reinforcements or at most 5 minutes will be necessary. Consult your instructor before proceeding to the next step. Record incidence of reinforcement consumption in Table 13-3 by tabulating as before.

STEP D. SHAPING

Now you are ready to begin the task of communicating to the rat the particular behavior you want it to do in order to obtain reinforcements. We "shape" or train the rat through a series of behaviors known as **successive approximation**. Starting with behavior only remotely resembling bar pressing, gradually shift to behaviors that come closer and closer to a true bar press. Wait until the rat is facing the bar and within a few centimeters, then deliver a reinforcement as in step C. Deliver the next one only after the rat is again a little closer than before. Continue this procedure of "coaxing" the rat to a point very near the bar. Then require it to stand up near the bar. For the next reinforcement, require the rat to touch the bar, then to push it a bit, and finally to press it to produce a click.

Keep a careful record in column 2 of Table 13-4 of the behaviors that have been reinforced at the start of shaping. This is a critical step. You must move forward to new, and closer, approximations fast enough to prevent fixation on one particular behavior, but not so fast as to "lose communication." Of the two possibilities, moving too fast is probably less serious because you can always go back and reinforce the preceding step once more. With skill, and a cooperative rat, you may complete shaping in 5 to 10 minutes. If the rat is not bar pressing in 25 minutes, consult your instructor for assistance.

Continue recording (i.e., tabulating) reinforcements on a minute-by-minute basis. Mark those tabulations that are clearly bar presses. You will likely find that some "almost bar presses" still need to be reinforced. Continue recording in Table 13-4 until you have a minute of all, or virtually all, true bar presses. When this occurs, shift immediately to step E.

If you succeed in getting the rat to press the bar in several tries, but not forcefully enough to produce a click, you may gently and quietly help press the bar with the rat. One or two times should be sufficient.

Special note: If step D has been completed in one lab period but you have to wait until the next period to start step E, you may need to go back and pick up (reinforce) earlier steps in the successive approximation before starting step E. This reshaping should require much less time. At the beginning of *every* lab day, give the rat 5 to 10 minutes of adaptation time before you begin the schedule for that day.

Step E. Conditioning

In step E, you will observe the increase in rate of the bar pressing response. The apparatus should be set so that a reinforcement is delivered each time the bar is pressed. This is called **continuous reinforcement**, or sometimes **CRF**. Do not allow reinforcements to accumulate in the magazine. Record bar presses on a minute-by-minute and cumulative basis in Table 13-5. Allow the rat 30

Operant Conditioning of the Rat

reinforcements. During this period, one of the experimenters should record every incidence of any of the four most frequent behaviors noted and tabulated in step A. After the rat has consumed the 30th reinforcement, discontinue conditioning at the end of that minute. Now go directly to step F without interruption, recording in the top half of Table 13-6. If the rat has not earned 30 reinforcements in 40 minutes, consult the instructor.

STEP F. EXTINCTION

Discontinue delivery of the reinforcement at the start of the next minute following the 30th response. Keep all other conditions the same. Record responses per minute as before and continue the observation of other behaviors. Continue this procedure for 10 minutes or until the rat fails to press the bar for 3 consecutive minutes, whichever comes first. At this point, write down the time shown on the clock. Very quietly and gently, remove the rat and place it back in its home cage. Avoid disturbing other groups as you leave the area. For those working with Sniffy, you can move directly to step I. Notice that a measure like **resistance to extinction** provides evidence for the strength of the conditioning. As you should see in step I and beyond, different schedules of reinforcement provide different response rates and strength of conditioning.

Sniffy

STEP G. DELAY PERIOD

During this time, you may work on the results collected so far. Copy data other experimenters have recorded, or begin graphing results, as explained in section 4. Exactly 20 minutes after your rat was placed in its home cage, return it to the Skinner box. Remember to be gentle and quiet.

STEP H. SPONTANEOUS RECOVERY

Again record responses per minute, this time in the bottom half of Table 13-6, but do not reinforce any response. Continue for 10 minutes or until you have 3 consecutive minutes of no response. Return your rat to its cage and clean up your lab room.

If the laboratory schedule permits another period on this project, teams of experimenters may elect to perform either steps I–J or steps K–L. In some sections, the instructor may assign the remaining work in order to vary the observations systematically.

Step I. Schedules of Reinforcement

Because the bar press response has been extinguished in your rat, you will need to recondition him although he might show spontaneous recovery when you return him to the Skinner box. After allowing some adaptation time, reinstate the conditions of step E. Begin these observations at any point where the rat spontaneously presses the bar. If he does not start bar pressing within 5 minutes, return to step D.

Common Schedules of Reinforcement

Schedule	Contingency	Rate of Response and Rate of Extinction
Continuous Reinforcement (CRF or RF-1)	Every response is reinforced.	Steady, moderately high rate of responding. Least resistant schedule of reinforcement schedule of reinforcement to extinction.
Fixed Ratio (FR-n)	Every nth response produces a reinforcement.	High rate of responding, with fairly short pauses after reinforcement. Moderately resistant to extinction.
Fixed Interval (FI-t)	The first response after a fixed time has passed is reinforced	Low rate of response, building up to reinforcement yielding a scalloped cumulative record. Moderate resistance to extinction.
Variable Ratio (VR-n)	The number of responses to gain a reinforcement varies with a mean of n.	Very high steady rate of responding, with no pause after reinforcement. High resistance to extinction.
Variable Interval (VI-t)	The time before a reinforcement varies about a mean of t.	Very steady and moderate rate of responding, without pauses. Moderate to high resistance to extinction.

Cumulative Response Records

FR-2   FI-3   VR-2   VI-4

Operant Conditioning of the Rat

Once the response begins, allow 10 consecutive reinforcements. This is a CRF (continuous reinforcement) or **FR-1** (**fixed ratio, one**) pattern, which means that every bar press is reinforced. Use Table 13-7 to record schedule of reinforcement effects. You will not need the center column, which is used by groups doing discrimination training. Circle tabulations where a reinforcement is given.

Switch from CRF to a different reinforcement schedule. Your instructor will advise you which type of schedule is practical to attempt here, or he or she may assign different schedules to different teams. You may find that you cannot make a big change all at once and may need to set the software or the system to work through intermediate approximations before establishing your final contingencies. Record every bar press and indicate those for which reinforcement was given. Continue for 20 minutes, then go to step J without a break.

Step J. Extinction

As in step F, discontinue reinforcement altogether but continue automatic recording, or use this condition for 30 minutes or until the rat fails to press the bar for 3 consecutive minutes. You can record using copies of Table 13-6 or make your own sheet. Following a Time Out, you might test for spontaneous recovery as before.

Although Sniffy has some advantages—for example he never gets satiated—he also has limitations. Now, it's time for Sniffy to rest as he cannot (yet) do discrimination learning or show other principles of learning such as stimulus generalization.

Step K. Discrimination

In discrimination training, you will be trying to "communicate" to your rat that it will be reinforced for a bar press under one stimulus condition (which we designate by S+, meaning stimulus present, and not reinforced for a bar press under another condition (designated S-, meaning stimulus absent). This is not an easy message for your rat to understand, particularly since it has poor vision and you will be using visual stimuli. (Auditory stimuli could be used, but these would be confusing to animals in other cubicles.) For these reasons, you need to be especially well prepared, quiet, and patient. Work with your cubicle in semi-darkness, with just enough light to see what happens and make recordings. Arrange for the *Controller* to turn on the panel light (S+) inside the cage above the magazine, and recondition the rat. After allowing some adaptation time (the rat is likely to show curiosity behavior toward the light), start conditioning with its first bar press; that is, reinstate the conditions of step E. If the rat does not start bar pressing within 5 minutes, return to step D. Once started, tabulate 10 bar presses in Table 13-7 and record the time required.

Turn off the light and discontinue the reinforcement for 2 minutes, as indicated by the light gray shading for S- in the center column. Continue to tabulate as before. Follow the schedule of S+ and S- periods as shown in Table 13-7. Your instructor may suggest that the duration of + and- intervals should be less than the 1-minute units indicated; for example, perhaps the intervals should be half minutes. It should be apparent that what you are doing is conditioning the bar press behavior when the light is on and extinguishing it when the light is off. One of the experimenters should record behaviors of the rat during the S- periods (in preparation for step L) as you did in step A. Continue this procedure for 40 minutes or until the rat shows a fair rate of responding in S+ conditions and not responding in 3 minutes of S- conditions. If after 40 minutes, the rat shows no differential behavior, consult the instructor. It may be desirable to use the overhead lights to indicate S+ and S- periods.

STEP L. CHAINING

Step L should not be attempted unless your rat has learned the discrimination in step K. The objective is to induce the rat to make a new response prior to pressing the bar each time. Thus, we will have a sequence (behavior x–bar press) or a chain of behaviors. The selection of behavior x is important. If you have good data on the behaviors of the rat during the S- periods of step K, select one of them as behavior x. If not, use your data from step A or consult the instructor . Keep lighting conditions the same as in step K and continue into step L without a break.

The procedure is essentially the same as in step D, shaping, except that you now use the panel light instead of the magazine click as a **secondary reinforcer**. Keep the light off until the rat approximates behavior x, then turn it on immediately. The rat

Operant Conditioning of the Rat

should be expected to go press the bar promptly and then go to the magazine for reinforcement. Turn off the light before the rat has a chance to return to the bar. Continue with this procedure, gradually requiring it to more closely approximate, and finally show, the desired behavior x. Tabulate behavior x and bar presses separately in a copy of Table 13-7 for 40 minutes or until a representative rate of the chained behavior is obtained.

4. Graphic Analysis of Results

Construct a cumulative curve of your rat's responses for the entire sequence of steps B through H. The appropriate identification for the abscissa is **minutes**, and for the ordinate, **cumulative bar presses**. Separate the various steps by drawing a vertical line from the abscissa to the top of the graph and identify these steps with an appropriate legend at the bottom. Because there are obviously no responses to record during step G, you may represent it with a double line just wide enough to contain the legend "Time Out," thus saving the graph paper space. Be sure the time scale properly allows for this time. Note also that you are graphing **cumulative** responses, so plan for the ordinate to continue to a value corresponding to the **total** number of responses in all of these steps combined. Below is a schematic representation of how your graph might look. Your data can be saved and loaded into your spreadsheet program, which might be useful in preparing your graph.

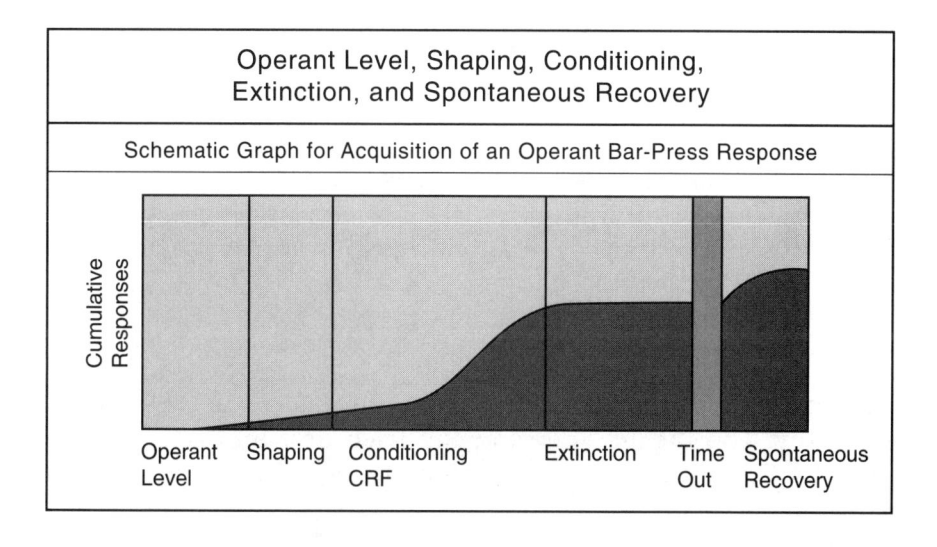

Operant Level, Shaping, Conditioning, Extinction, and Spontaneous Recovery

Schematic Graph for Acquisition of an Operant Bar-Press Response

Cumulative Responses

Operant Level | Shaping | Conditioning CRF | Extinction | Time Out | Spontaneous Recovery

Make a similar but separate graph to show the results of steps I–J, or, steps K–L, depending on what your team accomplished. For step I, draw the curves for all bar presses, whether reinforced or not, but indicate with a "tick" on the curve which ones were reinforced. For step K, draw two curves, one for S+ and another for S-. For step L, indicate where behavior x eventually appeared in final form (that is, the end of the shaping period).

5. SOCIAL INTERACTION (CONSULT YOUR INSTRUCTOR)

The use of animals in psychology is not restricted to the area of learning. Many psychologists use animals to investigate drug effects, underlying physiological correlates of behavior, and even social interaction. How would you predict that two trained rats in the same Skinner box would perform? They might establish a **dominance hierarchy**, where one animal becomes the "worker" and the other the "consumer." How long does it take to establish the hierarchy? What behaviors are characteristic during this period? What happens if two dominant animals are put together, or two submissive animals? How are we defining **dominant** and **submissive**? Do the rats exhibit the same types of behavior that you might predict of two people in a Skinner box?

6. PRECAUTIONS

Now that you have read and studied the entire procedure, we summarize the important aspects of successful conditioning. Keep these in mind at all times.

6.1

You must preserve quiet conditions. The rat is easily traumatized by noises we have learned to ignore. Speak in a low voice. Avoid moving chairs, tapping on the table, making noises with the apparatus. Sometimes even a ticking clock sitting on the table interferes with the rat's behavior.

6.2

Be familiar with your job so you can administer the experiment smoothly. The rat may become confused and uncooperative if there are unexpected shifts or irregularities in the sequence.

Operant Conditioning of the Rat

6.3

Do not continue any step longer than necessary to obtain the desired results. If the rat gets satiated, you cannot expect it to continue working for a reward.

6.4

When handling the rat, be very gentle and calm. Avoid sudden movements. The instructor will show you how to pick up a rat. Use no other method.

6.5

During periods when you are manually initiating reinforcement (step D and step L), timing is very important. Reinforcement must come promptly after the desired behavior, otherwise you are reinforcing something else and the result may be long delays in obtaining desired results.

6.6

In the animal room, follow the procedure described by your instructor. Under no circumstances should you interact with a rat other than your own.

7. INTERPRETATION

The following questions are for discussion, study, and review.

A. In what way can you consider conditioning a problem in communication? In this respect, is the situation between you and the rat substantially different from that which exists between parent and child or teacher and pupil in real-life training?

B. What do we mean by response probability? What is the difference in the probability of a bar press occurring in step B and at the end of step E? Can you structure some of your own learning in terms of response probability?

C. How does reinforcement modify response probability? How would you state the theory of reinforcement? What is the law of effect?

D. What happened to the alternative behaviors observed in step A during the various steps that followed? Did you observe the return of these behaviors in a later step? When? Why?

E. Suggest a situation in human training where successive approximation and conditioning could be used.

F. Explain in some detail why Skinner emphasized that in teaching an animal, you must "break up" certain kinds of unwanted behavior. In what way was this strategy used in the present experiment?

G. Compare results obtained by different teams. Is there any evidence for individual differences in behavior? Are these differences attributable to the rats or to the experimenters?

H. If different teams used different schedules of reinforcement in steps I–J, it is most appropriate to compare acquisition and extinction curves. Are there any striking differences? Can you explain why? Can you think of an everyday situation where the schedule of reinforcement is less than 100%?

I. Can you describe the process of learning to read in terms of discrimination conditioning and chaining?

J. Define the following terms introduced in this project: conditioned response, classical conditioning, operant or instrumental conditioning, competing behaviors, operant rate, response probability, cumulative responses, magazine training, shaping successive approximations, reinforcement, extinction, spontaneous recovery, reinforcement schedules (FR, VR, FI, VI, CRF), chaining, cumulative curve, differential conditioning (discrimination), generalization, contingent response, respondent behavior, intermittent reinforcement, secondary reinforcement, primary reinforcement, avoidance conditioning, and escape conditioning.

Student _____ Section _____ Due Date _____

OPERANT CONDITIONING OF THE RAT

1. Define the following terms introduced in this project:

Operant conditioning

Shaping

Reinforcement

Extinction

Secondary reinforcement

2. In animal conditioning, why do we start with magazine training? What is the role of the auditory click?

3. What does the angle or slope of the cumulative learning curve indicate about the rat's behavior? What does it mean when the curve is flat?

4. Write a report of the entire experiment, describing what you did and what your rat did. Avoid copying instructions from the manual, but tell it in your own words. Discuss any problems you had, how you solved them, and why they occurred. Imagine that you are writing for an intelligent friend, but one who was not present and never heard of operant conditioning.

5. Include any additional information your instructor requests.

6. Attach your graph(s) and the tables you used, properly labeled and annotated.

TABLE 13-1
BEHAVIORAL OBSERVATIONS

Observation Notes
First Minute:
Second Minute:
Third Minute:
Fourth Minute:
Fifth Minute:

Summary	
Most frequent behaviors:	Frequency
1.	
2.	
3.	
4.	
Total number of different behaviors	
Number of bar presses observed	

Operant Conditioning of the Rat

TABLE 13-2

OPERANT LEVEL OF BAR PRESS RESPONSE

Minute	Tabulation of Responses		Cumulative Responses	
	Bar Touches	Bar Presses	Touch	Press
1				
2				
3				
4				
5				
6				
7				
8				
9				
10				

TABLE 13-3

MAGAZINE TRAINING

Minute	Tabulation of Reinforcement Consumption	Cumulative Bar Press Responses
1		
2		
3		
4		
5		

TABLE 13-4
SHAPING THE BAR PRESS RESPONSE

Min-ute	Behaviors Reinforced in Shaping	Bar Press Tabulation	Cum. Resp.
1			
2			
3			
4			
5			
6			
7			
8			
9			
10			
11			
12			
13			
14			
15			
16			
17			
18			
19			
20			

Operant Conditioning of the Rat

TABLE 13-5

DEVELOPMENT OF THE CONDITIONED RESPONSE

Min-ute	Bar Press Tabulation	Cum. Resp.	Observations and Notes	Min-ute	Bar Press Tabulation	Cum. Resp.
1				21		
2				22		
3				23		
4				24		
5				25		
6				26		
7				27		
8				28		
9				29		
10				30		
11				31		
12				32		
13				33		
14				34		
15				35		
16				36		
17				37		
18				38		
19				39		
20				40		

TABLE 13-6

EXTINCTION AND SPONTANEOUS RECOVERY FOLLOWING CONTINUOUS REINFORCEMENT

Minute	Behaviors Observed in Extinction	Bar Press Tabulation	Bar Press Cum. Resp.
1			
2			
3			
4			
5			
6			
7			
8			
9			
10			

Minute	Behaviors Observed in Spontaneous Recovery	Time-Out Duration _____	Bar Press Tabulation	Bar Press Cum. Resp.
1				
2				
3				
4				
5				
6				
7				
8				
9				
10				

Operant Conditioning of the Rat

TABLE 13-7

WORKSHEET FOR SCHEDULE, CHAINING, OR DISCRIMINATION TRAINING

Minute	Bar Press Tabulation	Cum. Resp.+	Cum. Resp.−	S+ / S−	Minute	Bar Press Tabulation	Cum. Resp.+	Cum. Resp.−
1					21			
2					22			
3					23			
4					24			
5					25			
6					26			
7					27			
8					28			
9					29			
10					30			
11					31			
12					32			
13					33			
14					34			
15					35			
16					36			
17					37			
18					38			
19					39			
20					40			

PROJECT 14

CLASSICAL CONDITIONING OF EMOTION

The pleasant emotions of love, joy, belongingness, well-being, and surprise have their unpleasant counterparts in anger, sadness, anxiety, disgust, and fear. Studies of diverse cultures around the world show a remarkable similarity across our species to the registration, interpretation, perception, and recognition of emotions.

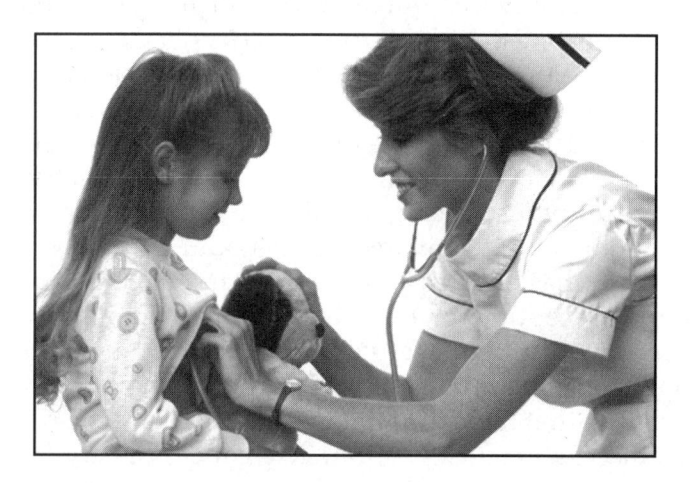

Our experience of emotion typically has a physiological component, where activation of the **autonomic nervous system**—specifically the sympathetic branch—intensifies our cognitive appraisal and labeling of our personal subjective emotion. This physiological component is important in that it promotes arousal and provides motivation to the organism. Sympathetic arousal results in increased heart rate, respiration, and blood pressure, and in a drop in skin resistance, among other physiological effects.

Classical conditioning of emotional and stress responses has become an important topic among the helping professions. **Health psychology** is the study of factors that affect our well-being, and stress is one of its main concerns. Health psychologists are often scientist-practitioners interested in a basic understanding of cognitive and neuropsychological processes affecting health as well as in how best to provide interventions and treatments.

In humans, measuring physiological functions that tell us about the state of various organ systems and their response to the arousal of the sympathetic nervous system is easy. One common measuring device is the polygraph. The **polygraph** has been used in psychophysiological measurement since the 1930s. Psychologists pioneered in the development of this instrument, which is used to measure a variety of biological signals, such as cardiac function, brain activity, muscle tension, and respiration rate. A polygraph consists of a transducer that allows biological activity to be converted into electrical activity. In the **electroencephalogram**, or **EEG**, for example, the movement of ions across cell membranes in the brain results in millivolt fluctuations. The usually silver electrodes of the transducer that are placed on the scalp act as "pick-ups" for these fluctuations. This small biological signal usually is amplified before it is reproduced on a display device such as a chart, oscilloscope, or computer cathode ray tube. The EEG has been a useful measure in a number of psychological situations. For example, it can show clinical abnormalities in brain activity. In **biofeedback** and relaxation therapies, patients are provided with information (feedback) on their brain wave activity so they can monitor the effect of various behaviors.

The **galvanic skin response**, or **GSR**, is a measure of small changes in electrical resistance of the skin. These changes generally correlate with **sympathetic nervous system** activity. The sympathetic nervous system is designed to prepare the body for "fight or flight" and is activated in stress and arousal. One use of the GSR, then, has been as a measure of arousal associated with detection of deception, or **lie detection**. Many American corporations and institutions use polygraph screening tests to make personnel decisions. The assumption is that the polygraph can detect arousal, that lying is arousing, and therefore the polygraph may be able to detect deception. The concept is controversial

Classical Conditioning of Emotion

for several reasons. For one, a psychopathic or, **sociopathic, personality** tends to show little sympathetic arousal when lying; hence such a person does not show the concomitant drop in GSR that might be expected. Ted Bundy, the mass murderer, felt no remorse and believed that his female victims were somehow at fault. He was not particularly emotionally aroused by a discussion of how or why he murdered them. Because sociopaths appear to be truthful, personnel managers may be selectively hiring these deviant personality types! Perhaps even more distressing is the "false positive" rate, where innocent people appear to be lying. If, for example, you were asked your name and then asked if you were a murderer, thief, or whatever, you might, not surprisingly, show more arousal to the second question than to the first. Thus innocent people may appear guilty and guilty people appear innocent. It's probably a good thing that polygraph data is not admissible in court.

Polygraph provides a sophisticated simulation of classical conditioning of the GSR, which in this case might be thought of as a galvanic silicon response modeling physiological arousal in the sympathetic nervous system. You can use the software to investigate the emotional and arousing properties of different English words and slang expressions. You can set up contingency pairings and generate detailed data on the **orienting response, habituation, delay conditioning, trace conditioning, backward conditioning, stimulus generalization, extinction,** and **spontaneous recovery**. Because this is an advanced project, you will use your own experience and understanding to develop experiments elucidating these basic principles.

There is good reason for you to do the hard work in this project to develop a deep understanding of the relationship between classical conditioning and emotion. **Stress** affects all of us, producing skin disorders, stomach symptoms, muscle problems, headache, fatigue, high blood pressure, heart problems, and changes in the immune system. In fact, it is estimated that as much as 50% of all hospital admissions are directly stress-related. How is it that certain otherwise harmless stimuli come to elicit stressful responses? Apparently, classical conditioning brings about such pairings. For example, driving on the road to work, even on a day off, is enough to dangerously raise the heart rate and blood pressure of some employees. In classical conditioning, a previously neutral stimulus (**conditional stimulus**, or **CS**) is paired with a stressor (**unconditional stimulus**, or **UCS**) so that eventually the conditional stimulus by itself can elicit the the stress response. Sometimes people misinterpret this relationship and think that it means that stress is "all in your head." On the contrary, these powerful and automatic conditioning effects cause real physiological change in many of the body's systems. For example, in the field of **psychoneuroimmunology**, classical conditioning can be used to produce an immune reaction to a neutral stimulus, like a light, simply by pairing it with an allergen (O'Leary, 1990). This may be the mechanism whereby psychological and cognitive factors play a triggering role in allergies, asthma, multiple sclerosis attacks, and other disorders that are sometimes referred to as urban or industrial "sickness."

To prepare for this project, read the chapters on learning in your text and look through the *MacLaboratory* stack called Classical Conditioning. Your challenge will be to set up the methods by which you will try to discover the factors affecting the "conditionability" of your computer using *Polygraph*.

1. PURPOSE

To demonstrate GSR arousal, habituation, and classical conditioning.

2. APPARATUS

Macintosh and *Polygraph* software.

3. PROCEDURE

The simulation assumes that Macintosh is a human being connected to a polygraph. Normally in polygraph recording, a number of functions, such as heart rate, blood pressure, respiration, and GSR are measured. The typical GSR measurements that you will take to plot the course of conditioning are latency, amplitude, and duration. These measurements will be stored in the application and you should save them periodically and then create a text file that can be opened for analysis and graphing by your spreadsheet program. To successfully investigate the various aspects of conditioning, expect to work for a couple of hours just collecting all your data. Some planning ahead can help. For example, how many pairings of the CS and UCS will you provide

Classical Conditioning of Emotion

before you test the CS alone? For this type of conditioning, 50 or more pairings to develop a well-conditioned response is not unrealistic.

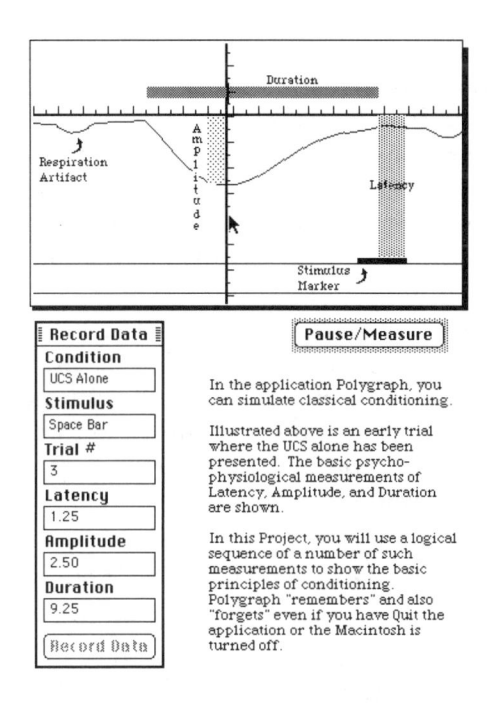

In the application Polygraph, you can simulate classical conditioning.

Illustrated above is an early trial where the UCS alone has been presented. The basic psychophysiological measurements of Latency, Amplitude, and Duration are shown.

In this Project, you will use a logical sequence of a number of such measurements to show the basic principles of conditioning. Polygraph "remembers" and also "forgets" even if you have Quit the application or the Macintosh is turned off.

If the computer were a normal human being, pictures, erotica, provocative language, fear, pain, or a variety of arousing stimuli would cause physiological activation of the sympathetic nervous system. The results would be increased heart rate, irregularities in respiration, and a drop in GSR. In this simulation, the program uses a series of algorithms based on the Rescorla (1988) model to give a humanlike GSR (here, GSR stands for galvanic silicon response). Use the keyboard or mouse to enter various stimuli. The "left arrow key" provides an unconditional stimulus to the computer. In a human, this would be equivalent to a mild electric shock or some other stressor. The "right arrow key" sends the computer the message that has been typed in the stimulus text field. The program knows the meaning of many English words and slang phrases, and responds accordingly. By pairing words or phrases, previously neutral stimuli come to be conditioned stressors activating arousal. Some words are already arousing to the computer, and it will remember and forget new things you may have taught it.

Classical Conditioning of GSR

3.1 Habituation

When you first start this program, you will notice that entering a neutral word stimulus causes a small arousal response on the part of your computer. In humans, we normally think of this as a novelty response that is sometimes called the **orienting reflex**. (At the risk of **anthropomorphizing**, your machine is "nervous" about this novel situation, and maybe you look and sound scary.) If you repeat the entry at short intervals, **habituation** occurs and **response amplitude** decreases. (Presumably the computer is less aroused and is settling into the situation.) If you were to turn the computer off and then start again, this change or alteration would likely be *dishabituating* and you would see the reappearance of the response. As with humans, some stimuli are more arousing than others. These stimuli take a long time to habituate, if ever. For example, if you type in "off-color" language you will find that the computer is always sensitive to such crudities.

3.2 Acquisition of a Conditioned Response

Pressing the "left arrow key" to record an unconditional stimulus does not lead to rapid habituation; in fact, it rarely leads to habituation at all. Other entries, however, like numbers, made with the "right arrow key," produce little, if any, GSR response. In psychological terms, we might say that the "left arrow key" is an unconditional stimulus that elicits an **unconditional response**. A number entered via the "right arrow key" is a neutral stimulus that elicits no response. If, however, you choose a specific number key, say 4, and pair it with the UCS, eventually 4 will become a **conditioned stimulus** and itself elicit a **conditioned response**.

Schematic Graph for Acquisition of a Conditioned GSR Response

Amplitude of GSR Response vs. Habituation | Conditioned Test Trials (Every 10th Trial CS Alone) | Extinction | Time Out | Spontaneous Recovery

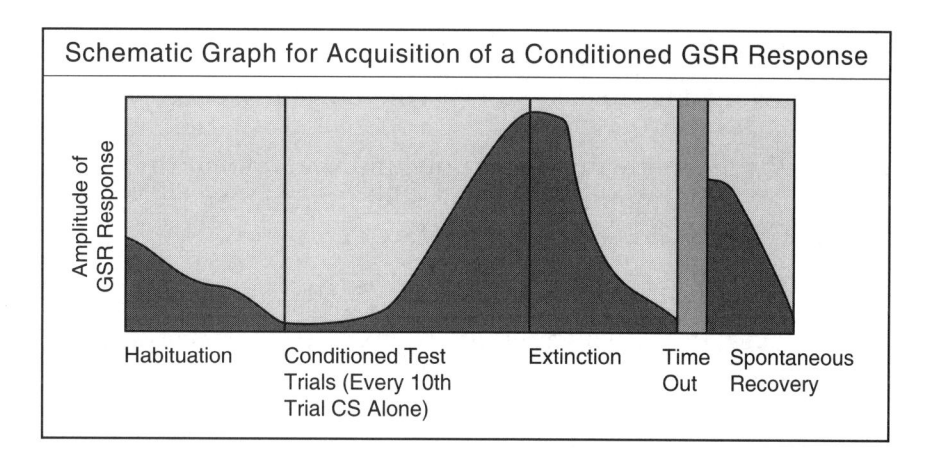

4. Data Analysis

Use an empirical method to discover:

4.1 Arousing Stimuli

4.2 Factors Affecting Habituation and its Time Course

4.3 Time Contingency Requirements for Conditioning

(Consider at least delay, trace, and backward conditioning.)

4.4 Magnitude Relationship Between the Unconditional Response (UCR) and the Conditioned Response (CR)

4.5 Number of Trials to Extinction Following Continuous CS-UCS Pairings

4.6 Spontaneous Recovery

4.7 Partial Reinforcement Effects

Make up tables or graphs to show your investigations of these phenomena. The application allows you to take actual measurements of time and amplitude from the computer screen. Data from your measurements should be saved as a text file so you can use your spreadsheet to plot tables and graphs.

5. Interpretation

The following questions are for discussion, study, and review.

A. Identify the following terms: polygraph, autonomic responses, classical conditioning, arousal, GSR, transducer, UCR, UCS, CR, CS, EKG, EEG, orienting reflex.

B. Why should we refer to the changes measured in this project as arousal rather than as emotion, anxiety, excitement, or some other term?

C. On what assumptions is the use of the polygraph in lie detection based? What are some of the limitations on its success as a "lie detector"? Why have the American Psychological Association and the U.S. government legislated against the use of lie detectors?

D. In this study, the data came from a single subject. Does the n necessarily restrict the experimenters' ability to make inferences? What is a repeated measures design?

E. Look up the Rescorla and O'Leary references and provide a brief review of them.

O'Leary, A. (1990). Stress, emotion, and human immune function. *Psychological Bulletin, 108,* 363–382.

Rescorla, R. A. (1988). Pavlovian conditioning. *American Psychologist, 42,* 119–129.

Student _____ Section _____ Due Date _____

CLASSICAL CONDITIONING OF EMOTION

1. Briefly describe your method of empirical observations, data collection, and results for the following aspects of the classical conditioning experiment, referring to your attached tables and graphs: delay, trace, backward conditioning, extinction, and spontaneous recovery.

2. Attach your tables and graphs, making sure they are clearly labeled and identified.

INTRODUCTION

SECTION 5

SENSATION AND PERCEPTION

Sensation is the conscious awareness of the stimulation of your sense organs. **Perception** is the awareness, organization, and interpretation of sensation. For example, the first time you see the following illustration, you are aware of the sensation of splotches of black and white. After a time, your brain organizes the information to make a more meaningful whole. You then see an animal in a picture. This principle of organization and interpretation we call perception—the animal is perceived. Once you have perceived an organization, it is virtually impossible to again see a complete lack of organization.

We seem to be born with some perceptual predispositions, like the recognition of a face. We seem to learn others, like **linear perspective** and **size constancy**. Still others are cultural-dependent. Unfortunately, in cases of brain injury we can also lose the organizing ability we call perception. For example, in **prosopagnosia**, individuals who have lesions of the right hemisphere near the parietal occipital boundary may lose the ability to recognize a face, even their own or that of a loved one. They can still see, they can still describe the person's eye color, beard, or whatever, but they don't perceive the whole.

As a general observation, damage to the right hemisphere often leads to **agnosia**, which might be thought of as sensation without perception or organization of the whole. A common neuropsychological screening test for right hemisphere function is to have a patient draw a clock. People with damage often produce a drawing that has the individual components of a clock, like hands and numbers, but they are not organized into a whole.

Introduction

For example, the entire left side of the clock might be left blank. Remember that the left side of the body and the left visual field are managed by the right hemisphere of the brain. As a general rule, all sensory and perceptual systems function in similar ways. Thus the patient with the right hemisphere lesion may also show **neglect** for tactile sensations from the left side of his or her body. In a case of neglect, it is as if the person doesn't perceive the wholeness of his or her own body or the surrounding environment. Such people are unlikely to put on the left sleeve of their shirt or the left leg of their pants. In other words, not only do we use our eyes to see, not only is the visual cortex of the occipital lobe our "vision center," but in fact our whole brain, past experience, everything, is brought together for our view of the world.

The study of sensation and perception tells us a great deal about the way the brain is organized. In this section, we present two quite different approaches that psychologists have used to study perceptual and brain processes. For vision, we emphasize a phenomenological approach and for audition we emphasize the psychophysical approach as research techniques.

In your software *Visual Perception*, you can explore a number of visual phenomena. A particular illusion or effect is meant to stimulate your thinking about how our brains are organized or about our perceptual capacities. The challenge for you is to devise and conduct an experiment to elaborate on the phenomenon or address some hypothesis. For example, use the following illustration to find your **blind spot**. You will need to get fairly close to the page, about the width of your palm. Close your right eye, and use your left to look at the eye on the page. By keeping your one eye fixated on the target and moving the book slightly closer or further, you should see the "apple" disappear. It appears to be missing because the image falls on that part of your retina where there are no visual receptors. The blind spot is the "hole" in your retina where blood vessels and nerves enter and leave the eye.

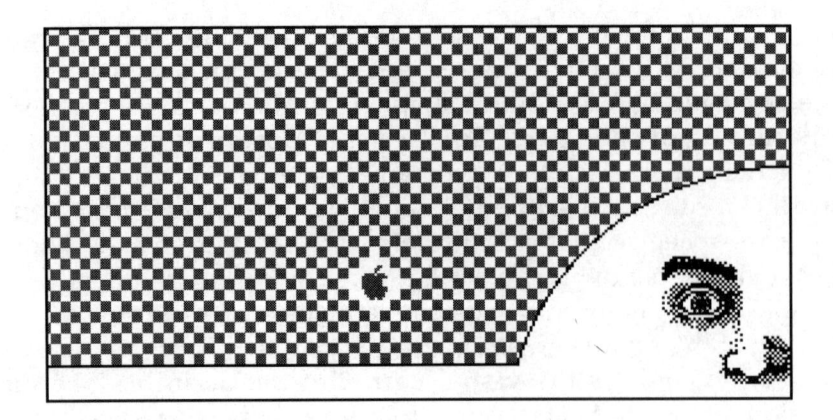

For our purposes, the point of this test is not simply that you learn that you have a blind spot—your textbook covers most of the "facts" about our visual systems. Rather, we want you to think about what that tells us about our brains. We normally don't notice the fact that each eye has a blind spot. Does this mean that one eye "cover" for the other to "fill in the blanks"? We can test that hypothesis by using just one eye. Do we now see a "hole" where our blind spot is located? No. So your brain is obviously "making up a little lie" about what is there. What exactly does it make up? Does it fill in the space with the surrounding background pattern? Does it keep the same brightness? Don't forget that your computer is a powerful psychology research tool that you can use if you've got a good idea for an experiment or can use to "play around" until you get a good idea and make an interesting observation. For example, you can use a color painting package to investigate if you have other "blind spots" for specific colors, and where those **color zones** might be. Because the periphery of the retina has few cones, you should be able to find areas where you cannot identify colored spots.

I was a student when I did my first real research experiment—that is, one that wasn't just a replication of some classic from the literature. It was very stressful to have to think up something entirely new. A number of my classmates basically just copied something else they had seen. But I wanted to try to do something really original. The area of sensation and perception seemed a good place to get an idea because you could try out ideas on yourself pretty easily before bothering anyone else. That's your challenge in this section. Try an original experiment in vision or hearing using your software.

You actually don't even have to use the computer, but it might be convenient. I didn't use it for my experiment. By the way, my experiment concerned the question of whether our sense of touch is "hard wired" into our brain or has to be learned. I thought it might have to be learned because of a lecture I had heard given by Dr. Donald Hebb. He thought at that time that sensory systems had to learn their perceptions. I figured that because we wore shoes a lot (it's pretty cold during school in Canada) our toes didn't have much chance for individual learning and therefore might not know exactly where they were being touched. I tested that hypothesis by lightly touching the second, third, or fourth bare toes of my subjects. They were my poor roommates and family. It turns out they didn't always know which toe was being touched, getting about 30% of the trials wrong. If I touched the first or fifth toes or gave them lots of feedback, they learned quickly but later forgot. I don't think anybody has done any experiments like this before or since. You might try something like it and if you do, let me know what you find out. For example, is it the same sort of thing when we twist our wrists around and clasp our hands together and interlock our fingers? You know, that sort of double-jointed kid's trick from grade school. Someone then points to a finger and you sometimes can't figure out which one to move.

PROJECT 15

DISCOVERING THE LIES TOLD BY YOUR EYES

Perception is an extraordinarily complex mental activity, where the brain attempts to construct a "logical" interpretation of the sensory information it receives. We usually become aware of this logical interpretation process when the brain is confronted with an illusion or some ambiguous sensory information. In other words, we catch our brain telling us a "little lie." For example, open the stack, Visual Perception, and press the Map button so you can easily go to the experiment card **Color Adaptation**. You will find the following discussion easier to follow if you actually use your software as you read along. The idea is to observe a phenomenon and then make and test some hypotheses about it. Start with the dark mask showing on top of the color red. Fixate on the target for about a minute, then without moving your gaze, click the button to hide the mask. You will see that the portion that was under the mask appears to be redder; that is, it has more **saturation**. We could hypothesize a number of reasons about why that occurred. We'll explore some possibilities here as examples of how you can use the software to study phenomonological aspects of visual perception.

The effect we observed in Color Adaptation might mean there is something special about the red receptor in the retina. Does the same thing happen if the stimulus is blue or green?

When the dark mask is hidden, it leaves an **afterimage** that has the effect of adding brightness to the previously covered region. Switch to the light mask and try the experiment again. This should add relative darkness to the region. These afterimage effects occur, but can you detect an increase in saturation or "richness" of the color in both cases independent of any afterimage-induced brightness effect? If not, then, can the effect be due only to afterimages? If you need to study up on afterimages, go to the Afterimages card and do some experiments there.

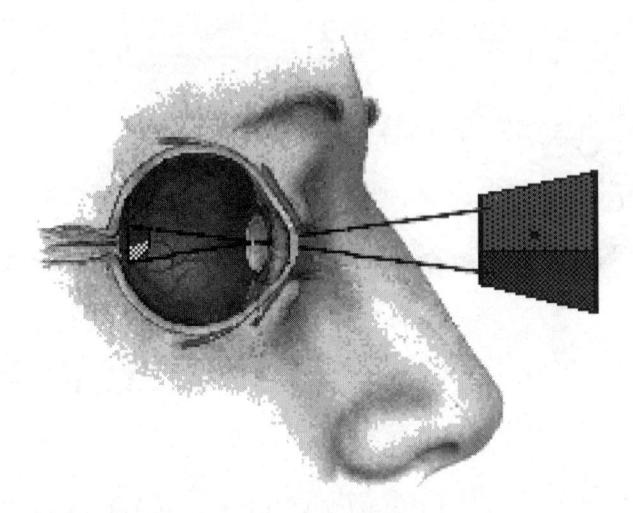

What is happening might be thought of as **color constancy**, which is conceptually similar to **size constancy** or the other constancies you have learned about in your text or in the stack. You might hypothesize, therefore, that fatigue is occurring for the red receptors in the exposed part of the stimulus. Our brain, however, "knows" that colors don't "fade"—after all, that would make it difficult to keep track of the tigers or other bad things from our evolutionary past. In other words, even though the physiological intensity of receptor activity might be decreasing due to the metabolic fatigue of the chemical reaction in the red **cones**, our brain interprets the color as constant in its three component dimensions of **saturation**, **hue**, and **brightness**. When the red receptors that are not fatigued behind the mask are suddenly exposed, they send a strong neurological signal that the brain interprets as a greater saturation of color. The brain is "caught in its little lie" about colors being constant. It then takes a moment to integrate the two apparent regions into a single homogeneous color. How long does it take for a "single" red color to reappear? How does this time compare with the persistence of an afterimage? If the phenomenon is based on the fatigue of receptors, does the amount of time you stare at the masked stimulus have any discernible effect on the magnitude or duration of the effect? How might illumination and contrast of your monitor setting affect the result? Presumably, if you turn down your monitor, the less intense light might make receptor fatigue take longer. Is this so? If you used a yellow stimulus, would there be a difference in effect because two receptors (red and green) are used to make up that color in your brain? Could this explain the **Purkinje shift**? Anyway, the point is to encourage you to think like a scientist: to observe a phenomenon and then to generate some hypotheses and test them. This is the essence of the empirical approach and is what permits us to escape the mental enslavement of superstitions and vacuous superficial conclusions.

The stack Visual Perception contains other examples of ambiguous sensory information, phenomena, and illusions for you to explore. For example, wearing 3-D glasses when you view the card **Retinal Rivalry** causes one pattern to be presented to one retinal field and a different one to the other retinal field. Most people with equally dominant eyes observe the predominant pattern shifting back and forth as each retina vies for dominance

A better known ambiguous stimulus is the **Necker cube**. A wire drawing of the cube can be interpreted by the brain as being in one of two orientations. If you look at it for a while the cube will alternate between orientations whether you want it to or not. Using the software you can perform an experiment while rotating the cube. For example, what effect does color have on the rate at which alternations occur? Does the angle of rotation affect alternations? You will notice that when a rotating cube apparently switches its orientation, the direction of rotation also appears to reverse.

As you look through the stimuli included in Visual Perception, find other examples of ambiguities and illusions that the brain interprets in its attempt to make sense of external reality. An understanding of why and how our brains lie to us is an important part of cognitive science and the study of "knowing." It should also alert you to the notion that although our brains encourage "seeing is believing," believing isn't necessarily the truth.

1. PURPOSES

To design, execute, and report on your own experiment in visual perception. To learn the fundamental concepts of color perception.

Visual Perception

2. APPARATUS

Macintosh computer with at least 16 levels of color and the Color Perception stack running under HyperCard. If color is not available to you, it is still possible to conduct some experiments.

3. PROCEDURE

Write a methods section and present a graph or table of your results for one of the following experiments. The first three do not require a color Macintosh. Make sure your methods section clearly details the independent, dependent and controlled variables you've established and describes how they have been operationally handled.

3.1 MUELLER–LYER ILLUSION

Use HyperCard's drawing tools to create stimuli of different proportions, as illustrated below. Present at least five subjects with a comparison figure for each. By having them use the "marquee" to select the comparison figure while holding down the command key, subjects can shrink or stretch so that it appears to match in length with the standard. Your dependent variable could be a count of the number of pixels subjects set for the comparison figure. Use Fat Bits under the Options Menu to get an accurate count. Graph the results to see if there is any observed difference between the "arrow" and "box" illusions.

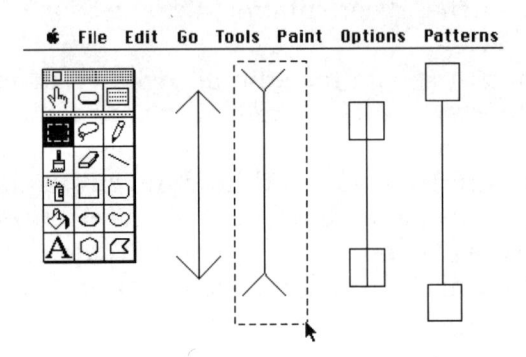

3.2 Autokinetic Effect

Look at the Observations field on the Autokinetic card and set up the environment with restricted illumination and field of view. With yourself as the subject, make at least five observations, separated by a rest period, of the length of time before apparent movement occurs. For your observations, select two distinct periods in your circadian rhythm, such as mid-morning and late in the evening. Graph your results.

3.3 Necker Cube Reversal

With yourself as subject, use both a stationary and a rotating Necker cube. Have it oriented vertically, horizontally, and on the diagonal for three different conditions of the independent variable. Run at least five 3-minute trials in each condition. Graph the number of reversals that appear to occur in each condition. How does rotation affect the reversal rate?

An alternative experiment might deal with the effects of color on the reversal of the Necker cube. Rotate the cube on the diagonal for five 3-minute trials for each of four colors. Choose two colors so that they match as closely as possible the wavelengths of optimal sensitivity to human red, green, or blue receptors. Choose the other two colors to have some intermediate wavelength value. Graph the effects of color on the rate of reversal.

3.4 Color Zones of the Retina

Use your painting program to investigate regions of the retina that are sensitive to the **primary colors**, as suggested by the discussion of the **blind spot** in the introduction to Sensation and Perception.

3.5 Purkinje Shift

For four different levels of brightness of your computer's monitor, plot the apparent change in RGB values for the four psychological primaries of red, yellow, green and blue. The RGB values could be achieved by making a subjective comparison using Color Picker in the Control Panel under the Apple menu. You will have to reset the monitor brightness to high in order to make the comparison.

3.6 RETINAL RIVALRY

Ask at least six of your classmates who showed variable differences in preferred and nonpreferred hand performance in Project 5 to participate. Have them use the 3-D glasses and record the length of time the right eye or the left predominates in a 10-minute session. Calculate correlations and plot scattergrams showing the relationship between strength of handedness (as operationally defined) and retinal dominance.

3.7 AFTERIMAGES

The study of afterimages can help us understand the "rules" used by the brain to mix colors. These rules of color mixture for light stimuli are not the same as for pigments. Be prepared to do some experiments to show that what you have learned since kindergarten about mixing paints does not hold true when it comes to mixing colored lights, or to considering color TVs or our visual systems. For example, yellow and blue pigments mixed give a green hue; mixing the same colors of lights yields a gray hue. Check out the card Color Mixture. With the increasing prevalence of electronic media that mix lights and not pigments, it is important that you understand the basic sensory processes involved.

Sensation and perception are interrelated. You can see this by conducting an experiment, for example, with the afterimage stimuli. When one color is stimulated, the **complementary color** is inhibited. The central nervous system, as a general rule, uses this process of excitation and inhibition to sharpen features in the sensory environment. The afterimage is thought to occur because the inhibited complementary color "rebounds" after the initial stimulus is removed. The **opponent processes** theory, first proposed by Hering in the last century, recognized what we know now: that the lateral geniculate and visual cortex are organized into complementary, or opponent, color processes. Anatomically, red and green, yellow and blue, and black and white form complementary pairs.

You can observe the interaction of sensation and perception by trying the following experiment. Fixate on the yellow stimulus window of the Afterimages card. Then switch to the neutral afterfield. In a moment, a blue afterimage, the complementary color of yellow, will appear. Go back and concentrate on the

Discovering the Lies Told by Your Eyes 245

yellow stimulus again, then select the red afterfield. The afterimage will appear purple as the brain interprets the blue afterimage as mixing with the red afterfield. Use the Afterimages card to show that the complementary color of red is green, of yellow is blue, and vice versa. Use the Color Mixtures cards to learn the principles of color mixture for lights. Why is it only with red, green, and blue color receptors in the retina (**trichromatic theory**) that we end up with an opponent process organization in the central nervous system?

For actual data collection, you might test subjects by making up mixtures in a color painting program of "interlaced pixels" and have the subjects choose "matching " resultant colors from the Color Picker. Do the same thing for afterimages. You can record the RGB values for numerical data.

3.8 Color Adaptation

Set up a series of experiments with the color adaptation phenomenon, as suggested in the opening discussion of this project.

3.9 Alternate Experiment

You may design and conduct your own experiment in visual perception. You might find that a painting or drawing program is useful to create stimuli. For some experiments—for example, **subliminal perception**—you might want to use the application Reaction Time, which comes with your software, for millisecond presentation of your stimuli and accurate response collection. You can quite easily make up stimuli with simple cut, copy, and paste commands from your painting program.

4. Interpretation

The following questions are for discussion, study, and review.

A. Define or identify the following: principles of color mixture for light and for pigments, color adaptation, color zones, gestalt principles, Purkinje shift, anatomy and physiology of vision, factors in depth perception, depth-dependent illusion.

B. Why are masks of different brightness provided for the color adaptation effect?

C. What effects does our past evolutionary history have on basic perceptual processes?

D. Why are we generally not aware of afterimages every time we look around?

E. Why, when we move our head rapidly, does vision not blur? What happens if you move a camera when taking a picture?

F. Distinguish between sensation and perception. What roles do learning and memory play?

G. What is meant by perceptual constancy? What examples are shown in the software?

H. How do attention, arousal, or emotion affect perception?

I. What are the perceptual capabilities of infants?

Student _____ Section _____ Due Date _____

Discovering the Lies Told by Your Eyes

1. Provide a detailed Methods section for your empirical investigations of a perceptual phenomenon.

2. Write a Results section and a brief Discussion section for your experiment. Attach your tables or graphs from your experiment.

PROJECT 16

JUST HOW WELL DO YOU HEAR?

Sound travels to our ears in the form of a wave transmitted through the air. When we see the starship Enterprise blasting some object in space, there should be no sound since there is no air. We are a Terra-centric species, however, and thus we like our fantasies to appear "real," so the movie people add in the sounds of explosions, background "mood" music, and so forth. When a sound wave enters our ear, it is transduced into a mechanical wave in the **basilar membrane** of the **cochlea** in the inner ear. Hair cell receptors then send a signal along the **eighth cranial nerve** to the **auditory cortex**. This signal contains neurally coded information about the original wave. In this coding, the **wave amplitude** is interpreted as **loudness**, the **wave frequency** is interpreted as **pitch** (e.g., a high or low note), and the **wave purity** is interpreted as **tone** or **timber**. *MacLaboratory* contains the application Pitch, which includes a tone generator so you can experiment with the effects of amplitude, frequency, and wave purity on your auditory perceptions.

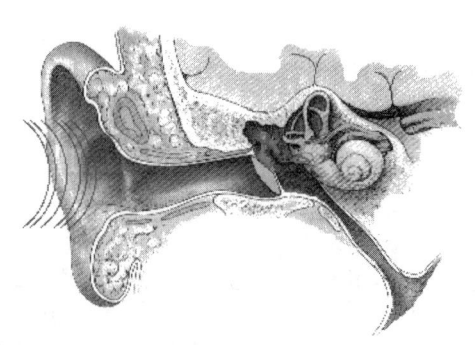

In general, **psychophysics** is the study of the relationships between the physical properties of stimuli and their psychological perceptions. In neuropsychology, we use tests to evaluate the capabilities of a person's sensory systems. For example, in hearing, we might measure the **absolute threshold**—that is, the lower and upper limits of the range of hearing. College-age students typically can hear sounds whose wave frequency is between 30 and 18,000 Hz. By the time these students reach old age, their hearing thresholds will be about 80 to 6000 Hz, or even worse if they have had significant industrial or rock music exposure.

In fact, thresholds are a matter of probability. Any stimulus may or may not be detected depending upon attention, motivation, or other factors. Thus, we generally use a 50% rule, where a threshold is established if a subject can correctly detect a stimulus with an accuracy that is 50% better than chance. Thus, if we were to say that your absolute lower threshold were 30 Hz, we would be saying that you could detect such a sound half of the time. A stimulus that is detected less than 50% of the time, but that is still occasionally detected, is a **subliminal stimulus**.

Psychophysicists have developed a number of methodologies to establish empirically whether a subject can detect a stimulus. For example, absolute threshold appears to vary depending on the direction of approach. If you started with a detectable sound—say of 40 Hz—and decreased the frequency on successive trials, you might get to 25 Hz before the sound was no longer detected. If you started up from the bottom, however, you might get to 35 Hz before a sound was detected. Thus, in the **method of ascending and descending limits**, both directions of approach are used in the trials.

Because this is an advanced project, it will be your responsibility to look at the details of the methodology used. You can do this by looking through the software pages of the experiments while in editing mode. In this case, we are doing an experiment to discover your **difference threshold** for pitch—that is, your ability to detect a change, for example, from 512 to 514 Hz. Obviously accurate pitch determination would be of interest to piano tuners and musicians. It should also be of interest to you as a measure of your auditory health.

Measuring the difference threshold also tells us about a basic perceptual process in the brain. Within the normal hearing range, the **just-noticeable difference**, or **JND**, is not a simple constant. Thus, if you can just notice the difference between 512 and 514 Hz,

Just How Well Do You Hear?

you cannot tell the difference between 1024 and 1026 Hz. In fact, **Weber's law** suggests that you would just notice the difference at 1028 Hz. In other words, the increase in amount or intensity of a stimulus producing a just-noticeable difference is proportional to the intensity of the initial stimulus. In fact, you might test to see whether Weber's law applies to other aspects of hearing besides pitch. Within the limits of your computer's sound capabilities, you might try finding JND's for loudness or tone. Does Weber's law hold for other senses such as vision or touch? Can you construct an IRP to test this?

1. Purposes

To determine the individual difference threshold for pitch and to illustrate one of the psychophysical methods. To investigate Weber's law.

2. Apparatus

Macintosh and the Pitch Discrimination application using the experiment files Pitch 256, Pitch 512, and Pitch 1024.

3. Procedure

Tones will be heard in pairs, and the two tones of a pair will differ in pitch. Sometimes the second tone, the test tone, will be higher in pitch and sometimes it will be lower in pitch than the first tone, the standard tone. The two tones will never be equal in this experiment.

The various pairs of tones heard will differ in their pitch separation; some will be very close together (and therefore difficult to distinguish) and others will be far apart and easy to distinguish. To make use of the precision inherent in the psychophysical method of just-noticeable differences, we order the pairs of tones in a systematic manner. Starting with a pair that is easily distinguishable, you will hear successive pairs of increasing difficulty (decreasing pitch difference) until we get beyond the point where you can distinguish them accurately. Then we will approach your threshold from the opposite direction by presenting a very difficult pair with successive pairs decreasing in difficulty (increasing in pitch difference). This pattern of alternating the increasing and decreasing series, the method of ascending and descending limits, will continue throughout the entire testing procedure.

For each pair of tones, you must guess if you do not know for sure. If the second tone is lower in pitch than the first, click on "Lower." If the second tone is higher in pitch, click on "Higher." Notice that a **confidence rating scale** is provided.

After testing is completed, the data display window will indicate your responses as well as the actual frequencies. Save your data as both a text file and an experiment file. Use a spreadsheet application to open the text file, and prepare and print a table appropriate for this experiment. The table should show your percentage correct at each of the difference levels. Test yourself at each of the three standard frequencies: 256, 512, and 1024. Excel macro files have been included in the software if you can use them.

4. Descriptive Analysis of Results

Construct a graph of your individual percentages correct by plotting frequency differences on the abscissa and percent correct on the ordinate. To find your own difference threshold for pitch, use the method of **linear interpolation**. From the 75% point on the ordinate, draw a line horizontally to the point where it intersects the curve. Then draw a vertical line from that point to the abscissa. Read the threshold from this intersection. If the 75% line crosses a curve more than once, find all of the values and obtain an average. If a curve is entirely above the 75% line, then the threshold is better (lower) than the test is designed to measure. If a curve is entirely below the 75% line, then the threshold is worse (higher) than the test is designed to measure. In either of these latter two cases, you may wish to construct new test files using the editing capabilities of this application to determine your actual thresholds. By the way, you should understand why 75% is used. If the difference threshold is defined as 50% better than chance, and chance is 50%, then the threshold needs to be measured at the 75% correct point.

5. Interpretation

The following questions are for discussion, study, and review.

A. What is your own difference threshold for pitch? Is it better or not as good as that for the entire class? Would you have guessed this from your knowledge of your musical ability?

B. Having calculated a Weber ratio, how do you apply it?

C. Compare your accuracy of pitch perception with a few others. Do differences relate in a systematic way with your past history of exposure to basilar membrane–damaging noises of 110 dB or more?

D. State the independent and dependent variables in this experiment.

E. Distinguish between an absolute pitch threshold and a difference pitch threshold.

F. How might your performance on this test of pitch discrimination relate to musical ability? How might it relate to music appreciation? Can you structure pitch discrimination ability as a **necessary** or as a **sufficient** prerequisite for musicianship?

G. List all the potentially confounding variables and describe how they were controlled. Were the control procedures adequate?

H. What are the limitations of Weber's law?

I. What difference in analysis and interpretation occurs in designs where one subject is repeatedly measured, compared to a single measure for each of many subjects?

J. What is a decibel? Why do we measure loudness in decibels? What are your local or regional laws regarding noise pollution?

K. Discuss the frequency theory and the place theory as they relate to pitch.

L. How do we localize sounds?

M. What are the different types of deafness? How are they caused and how are they treated? Why do some deaf people believe they belong to a separate culture? Is American Sign Language just like English, except transmitted by hands? What obstacles do deaf people face in our culture?

Just How Well Do You Hear?

Student _____ Section _____ Due Date _____

THE DIFFERENCE THRESHOLD FOR PITCH

1. Determine your own Weber ratio by using the following formula for each of the three standard pitches:

$$\frac{\text{Threshold}}{\text{Standard}} = \underline{\hspace{4cm}} =$$

Are your data consistent with Weber's law?

2. Answer question ___ from the Interpretation section of this project.

3. Attach copies of your spreadsheet tables and graphs.

INTRODUCTION

SECTION 6

PERSONALITY AND SOCIAL PSYCHOLOGY

The first three projects in this section address three major approaches to personality: Freudian psychodynamic theory, social learning theory, and trait theory. How do we measure personality? How do you construct a survey of attitudes and opinions? The fourth project covers the use of surveys and questionnaires as a methodology common to **social psychology** and personality theorists.

The **psychodynamic theory** of personality emphasizes the dynamic interplay between the biological forces that Freud believed were our primary motivators and the moral values and social standards that form our good conscience. Freud thought of such biological drives as feeding, foraging, fighting, and sex as emanating from a pleasure-seeking domain of our personalities he called the **id**. The id is thought to reside in our **unconscious** mind. The id is more than simple selfishness; rather, it is a source of psychic energy from deep and "forbidden" thoughts of aggression and sexuality. In contrast to the id is the **superego**, which resides primarily in the **conscious** mind. Through the superego we become perfectly aware of society's expectations and prohibitions. Freud believed that the conflict between the incompatible demands of the id and the superego are juggled by the **ego**. The ego deals with reality and develops a number of mechanisms that allow it to make trade-offs in such internal conflict. For example, one **ego defense mechanism** is called **displacement**. Suppose you scold your child and the child is then angry with you. Your child's id advocates aggression. The superego points out all the prohibitions against aggression, as a good conscience should. The ego comes up with a trade-off, an emotionally expressive response that is socially acceptable—perhaps leaving and slamming the door. This displacement of aggression has allowed the ego to balance the competing demands.

Normal individuals exhibit a number of ego defense mechanisms. One common one is **repression**, where the ego tries to control uncomfortable desires or conflicts by keeping them buried or repressed in the unconscious. How might you test such a theory? Dr. Edward O'Brien and Dr. Jean O'Brien have devised a psychodynamic activation protocol that presents subliminal stimuli intended to activate repressed thoughts or ideas. Such thoughts should be more difficult to access and therefore show longer reaction times. These researchers feel that a good **counseling**

Introduction

psychologist or **clinical psychologist** should be employing scientific principles to validate underlying theories and constructs. One of the underlying assumptions of **psychotherapy** is that the therapeutic process allows inappropriately repressed experiences to be brought to consciousness, where they can be dealt with.

The project by my colleagues Toni Welch and Dr. Eric Zillmer regarding Nazi personalities can be viewed as a type of **social learning theory** issue. Were the Nazis more or less ordinary people for whom a variety of social and cognitive processes came together in such a way that they were made capable of committing the Holocaust and other atrocities? If so, it would imply that social learning factors can produce extremes in human behavior. Alternatively, were the Nazis psychologically disturbed individuals with abnormal neuropsychiatric functioning who just happened to come to power in Germany in the 1930s? If this is the case, it would imply that there might be a personality **trait** that embodies fascist characteristics. To investigate these possibilities, you will do a case study of Hermann Goering, a leading Nazi. The case workup includes your doing some content analysis on Goering's actual responses to a **Rorschach inkblot** test of personality. You then use a sample version of the modern *Diagnostic and Statistical Manual of Mental Disorders*, 4th edition (**DSM-IV**) of the American Psychiatric Association to determine if Hermann Goering meets the **diagnostic criteria** for a **delusional disorder**, or **schizophrenia**.

As an example of an objective personality test, our colleague Lauren Montenegro presents a simplified student-oriented version of a Type A/B test. **Trait theory** suggests that personality structures are composed of a group of relatively stable and enduring behavioral predispositions called traits. Type A/B may be thought of as a lifestyle trait that indicates how punctual or hardworking or conscientious a person might be. Type A behaviors also include negative emotions like anger, hostility, and depression. Individual traits are often linked together in clusters or groupings like this. Using the statistical procedure of **factor analysis**, researchers have identified a group of five main factors. These are often labeled **openness to experience, conscientiousness, extraversion, agreeableness,** and **neuroticism**. As a mnemonic strategy, you might notice that the first letter of each factor spells OCEAN. Although there have been some equivocal studies, for the most part Type A behavior seems to be an independent risk factor in heart disease. Interestingly, patients who receive special Type A counseling can significantly reduce their cardiac risk factors. In health psychology, the interaction of personality and physiology; the interaction of social factors, learning, and stress; and the interaction of development and environment all contribute to our overall well-being.

PROJECT 17

SUBLIMINAL PSYCHODYNAMIC ACTIVATION

EDWARD J. O'BRIEN, MARYWOOD COLLEGE
JEAN P. O'BRIEN, KING'S COLLEGE

Psychologists have, for many decades, sought ways to scientifically validate Freud's theories. Freud and many of his followers have argued that case studies of patient "cures" are acceptable scientific proof. Today, though, nearly all psychologists doubt the scientific validity of such a subjective approach and have developed more rigorous experimental methods to test Freudian theory. One of the most widely used and controversial methods is called the **subliminal psychodynamic activation** paradigm, which was developed by Lloyd Silverman and his colleagues. This paradigm studies unconscious processes by presenting stimuli at or below the threshold of awareness. These subliminal stimuli are used to activate the dynamic processes that should result in effects supporting Freudian theory. For example, an **Oedipal** process might be activated by presenting stimuli such as "Beating Dad is wrong." Subjects who experience such activation may then become less willing to compete with other males. Some studies (e.g., Silverman, Ross, Adler, & Lustig, 1978) find evidence for these hypotheses whereas other studies have difficulty replicating such findings (e.g., Heilbrun, 1980).

Some clinical psychologists believe that understanding unconscious processes is an essential element of therapy. They feel that the therapeutic process should help the individual recognize underlying conflicts and anxieties and permit them to be brought up to conscious awareness to be dealt with.

In this project you experience stimuli presented at the "edge of perceptual awareness." The limitations of a computer screen display make it impossible to present truly subliminal stimuli. Thus, you may see some of the stimuli clearly, others less clearly, and some not at all. Some stimuli represent "conflict" areas identified by psychoanalysts and other stimuli are not generally related to these presumed conflict areas. Because the experiment uses a within-subjects design that is sensitive to correct sequencing, it is best to go through the session and collect your data (sections 1-3 below) before you move to section 4 and data analysis.

1. Purposes

To examine the influence of different types of stimuli presented near the threshold of awareness. To examine the subliminal psychodynamic activation paradigm. To interpret results of an experimental test of Freudian theory.

2. Apparatus

Macintosh computers with the Hemispheres experiment files Subliminal Practice and Subliminal Test. Use the Subliminal Scoring Macro in Excel to complete your data collection and summary. If you do not have the Excel program, your instructor will provide hand-scoring templates for data analysis.

3. Procedure

You will run two sessions with yourself as a subject. The first session is a brief practice session that will acquaint you with the subliminal task; the second session presents the actual test. During both sessions, be sure to pay close attention to the center of the computer screen. Words will appear that are slightly removed from the center of the screen (i.e., up and to the left of center, up and right, down and left, down and right). Your task is to identify these words and type them in as quickly as possible. After the word goes off the screen, you will be prompted with a keyboard cue. Use the regular keyboard on the Macintosh to type in the word you saw, then hit the Return key. Note that *you are being timed*, so type the word you saw quickly and hit Return to stop the clock. Even if you are not sure of what you saw, type in your best guess. Accurate scoring depends on your entry of the word you saw or your best guess. The subliminal test is designed to present words at the edge of awareness, and often you may have seen more than you might think. Do not worry about matching upper- and lowercase letters.

Open up the file Subliminal Practice, which contains 16 practice trials. Our purpose in running this is to be sure you are "warmed up" and understand the procedures. To begin the practice trials, go to the Experiment menu and choose Run. Be sure that you are ready to proceed because the first stimulus will appear promptly. Remember, *be sure to type in the words you see and hit Return as quickly as possible*. Once the 16 trials have ended you may look at the stimuli and responses to see how you did. Close the file (do not bother to save the practice data).

If you have questions, check with your instructor before proceeding to the actual Subliminal Test. When you are ready, open Subliminal Test and again choose Run under the Experiment menu to begin. After the 64 test stimuli have been presented, choose Save under the File menu to save your data. A dialog box appears, as in the illustration below. Type in a code name (do not use your real name unless instructed to do so by your instructor). Select the Data Only (TEXT Format) option so that your data are saved in the correct format, which can be analyzed later in Excel. After you click on Save, you will see a prompt which says that Data Only (TEXT Format) files cannot be read by the application. Click O.K. since you will later be using Excel for subsequent analyses.

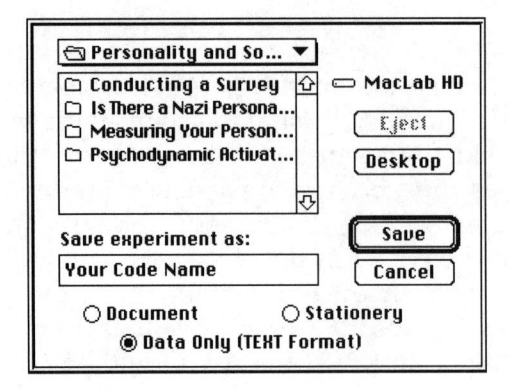

Once your data have been saved, Quit the Hemispheres program. You will be prompted to save an experiment file, but you need not do so for this experiment.

4. DATA ANALYSIS

This next session assumes you have access to Microsoft Excel to analyze your data. If you do not have this program, your instructor will provide you with a scoring sheet and directions you can use to calculate the results by hand.

To analyze your data, open up the Excel file Subliminal Scoring Macro. If you have a newer version of Excel, just click the button that appears and follow the instructions to find your file and summarize your data.

If you have an older version, open the Subliminal Test file you saved (recall that the file was saved under a code name you made up). If you are using System 7 or Multi-Finder, be sure to open your data file from Excel (i.e., while in Excel, pull down the File menu, select Open, and then select your data file). If you can't find the file, you may have forgotten to save it as a Data Only (TEXT Format) file. If this is the case, open up your experiment file in the Hemispheres program and save it again under the correct format. To begin the analysis with the older version, be sure that your data file is the top window of Excel and that the Subliminal Scoring Macro is open in a background window. Choose Run from under the Macro window, then choose *'Subliminal Scoring Macro'!Record 1* and click OK. The macro will organize your results and calculate and plot out the means for five categories of words: oral, anal, sexual, aggression, and control.

For all users, once the macro has run, print out the three-page summary of your results. It is easier to examine your printout later if you print in horizontal rather than vertical mode (set this under Page Setup in the File menu). After you have printed out the table, print the graph in a full-page view by double-clicking on the graph of response latencies so that it fills the screen and then selecting Print. Note that the x-axis of this graph includes the types of words in the subliminal study and the y-axis refers to mean response latencies (in secs). After the graph is printed, close the full-page view and then, in the Excel file, before you Quit, save the changes made.

At the top of the first page of the data sheet, near the center, there should be four sections labeled "Word Category," "Response Latencies," "# of Errors," and "Unusual Associations." Note that the response latencies have already been calculated and graphed for the five categories of words.

Calculate the "# of Errors" for each of the categories and enter these values in the appropriate row for oral, anal, sexual, aggression, and control words. Note that the macro has organized the words with borders around each category. Simply check to see if your response matched the stimulus and, *if not*, write in the value 1 under the "Error Count" column on the right side of the printed results. Be sure to include a response as an error even if you only missed a single letter. Calculate the number of errors in each word category and write the sums at the top of the page under "# of Errors."

Finally, note any "Unusual Associations" in the columns provided on your data sheet. For example, if your response to "Sex" was "Mommy" or "Daddy," this might be noteworthy.

4.1 INDIVIDUAL DESCRIPTIVE ANALYSIS

Now we consider how well your results match a Freudian hypothesis. Freud's theory, as described in your text, argues that we retain as adults unconscious remnants of early childhood conflicts and that adults have particular difficulty dealing with drives having to do with sexual, aggressive, anal, and oral concerns. The paradigm we are using suggests that conflicts in these areas will show up in the form of longer response latencies and in response errors. For example, if you have hang-ups about sex, the subliminal paradigm hypothesizes that it will take you longer to respond to sexual stimuli and that you will more often misperceive the cues associated with sex. In this paradigm we examine differences in response latency of 1/100th of a second; that is, the software will record differences in response that are only 1/100 of a second apart.

Examine the table and graph of your mean response latencies for each of the categories of words. The Freudian hypothesis contends that the conflict areas of sex, aggression, anal, and oral stimuli will have longer response latencies than will the control stimuli. Summarize your own findings and consider how they support or contradict the hypothesis.

Note several things. First, the words in the five categories were similar in length (that is, the average number of letters was 5.0 for each category). Also, the stimuli were presented in random order. In addition, because we used a within-subjects design, subject variables like intelligence, typing ability, and sex were controlled variables. Finally, equal numbers of words from each category were presented in each of the four presentation locations. Why is it important to present the stimuli in random order rather than presenting the oral words first, then the anal words, and so on? How might differences across categories in word length, order of presentation, or screen placement confound interpretations of the results of the experiment?

Consider the number of errors you made in recognizing the conflict and control words. For ease of computation, we will conduct a **chi-square** analysis of these two broad categories rather than considering each specific category. The chi-square statistic tests the hypothesis that the number of errors you made is equally distributed between conflict and control stimuli. In much the same way that we might evaluate whether a coin is loaded to land more often on heads or tails, we examine whether your errors of perception were more frequent with the conflict or control stimuli. Freudians would, no doubt, expect us to misperceive more often words that are associated with conflict and anxiety. A more detailed discussion of chi-square appears in Project 20 of this manual, but, if you are able to handle the following instructions, you do not have to read it now.

To calculate chi-square, you first need to count the total number of errors (regardless of category). If chance alone were operating to determine which words were misperceived, the expected number of errors for the conflict and control words would be the same (since there were an equal number of conflict

Subliminal Psychodynamic Activation

and control stimuli). The expected frequency of errors for the conflict and control groups is therefore the total number of errors divided by 2. For example, if you made 20 errors in the Subliminal Test, chance alone would dictate that 10 of these errors were on conflict words and 10 on control words.

To solve the chi-square equation, we use the following formula:

$$\text{chi-square:} = \Sigma \frac{(Y_i - E_i)^2}{E_i}$$

In words, we can solve this formula as follows:

1. For the *conflict words only*, subtract the expected number of errors (E_1) from the observed number of errors (Y_1) and square the difference.

2. Divide the result you found in step 1 by the expected number of errors for the conflict words (E_1).

3. Now, *for the control words only*, subtract the expected number of errors (E_2) from the observed number of errors (Y_2) and square the difference. (Note that the expected number of errors for the control words is the same as for the conflict words and that the sum of these two expected numbers ($E_1 + E_2$) should equal the total number of errors you made.)

4. Divide the result you found in step 3 by the expected number of errors for the control words (E_2).

5. Sum the results of steps 2 and 4 to obtain the chi-square value.

6. If the value you obtained is greater than 3.84, we can have statistical confidence that you made more errors in one category or another. Note whether your errors were more common for the conflict or control words, or if your errors were equally distributed across these two groups.

4.2 GROUP ANALYSIS

As has been described in earlier projects, to scientifically test an hypothesis such as the subliminal activation hypothesis we must examine information from groups to determine whether the findings you obtained individually are true more generally for a larger sample. To do this, you will provide your instructor with 10 bits of data dealing with your response latencies and error rates for each of the word categories. (This information should be located at the top of the printout of your results from the subliminal test; enter this information on a form your instructor will provide.) With this information, your instructor may conduct analyses such as an **analysis of variance (ANOVA)** to evaluate whether the subliminal activation hypothesis is supported by data from your class. If your school uses statistical software, you may be asked to do such an analysis yourself.

5. INTERPRETATION

The following questions are for discussion, study, and review.

A. Freudian theory emphasizes the centrality of **unconscious** factors in determining behavior. While it is, in principle, extremely difficult to observe unconscious factors, we can be aware of conscious factors that influence our behavior. Were you aware of any **conscious** factors, such as embarrassment or concern with evaluation, that influenced your behavior while participating in the subliminal study? Such conscious factors may serve as well as, or better than, unconscious factors in explaining the findings obtained.

B. Can you identify possible confounding variables that might have influenced the pattern of means produced by your data? That is, do any factors other than the content of the words (conflict versus control) account for the differences in latency?

C. Can you think of any groups of individuals who might have more or less difficulty in responding to the conflict words used in the subliminal study? For example, a sex therapist might be less defensive about sex words; a person with violent tendencies might be particularly defensive regarding aggressive words. Can you think of other types of stimuli that might be uniquely stressful for particular groups (e.g., pictures of guns and victims of violent crime)?

D. Did any of your responses seem humorous or unusual? What in your responses was humorous or unusual? Were such responses more common in any of the categories of words? If so, what is it about these categories that leads them to be associated with humor? How might Freud interpret such humorous or unusual associations?

E. How large was the difference in mean response latency between the category of words for which your responses were quickest and the category for which your responses were slowest? What are the implications of differences of this magnitude?

F. Why is it important that the words used in this project were presented in random order and that across the five categories the words had the same average number of letters? What other factors do you think need to be controlled in order to enhance the validity of this study?

G. Is the subliminal activation paradigm used in this project a fair test of Freudian theory? What might be done to test Freud's theory more directly? In taking a Freudian approach to personality, what are the advantages and disadvantages of analyzing data from individuals versus aggregating data for group analyses?

H. What are **ego defense mechanisms**? Which ones might be used to explain your results? Why do we have them?

I. Based on the project and class readings, is it possible to test Freud's theory experimentally? Is this theory scientific in nature or more based on Freud's beliefs, or worldview?

6. References

Burger, J. M. *Personality*. 3d edition. Belmont, CA: Wadsworth, 1993.

Heilbrun, K. S. (1980). Silverman's subliminal psychodynamic activation: A failure to replicate. *Journal of Abnormal Psychology, 89*, 560–566.

Silverman, L. H., Ross, D. L., Adler, J. M., and Lustig, D. A. (1978). Simple research paradigm for demonstrating subliminal psychodynamic activation: Effects of Oedipal stimuli on dart-throwing accuracy in college males. *Journal of Abnormal Psychology, 87*, 341–357.

Student _____ Section _____ Due Date _____

SUBLIMINAL PSYCHODYNAMIC ACTIVATION

1. Describe the critical features of the subliminal psychodynamic activation paradigm. Imagine you are writing that part of an abstract that deals with methods.

2. Write a Results section, including both latency and error data obtained in the subliminal study.

3. Write a Discussion section specifically indicating how well your data support, or fail to support, Freud's theory.

4. Identify both conscious and unconscious factors that may have influenced your results. Be specific with regard to your own experience and observations while completing the study.

5. Describe the difficulties involved in testing aspects of Freud's theory that deal with the unconscious.

6. Include any additional material your instructor may require.

7. Attach printouts of your spreadsheets (or hand-scored tables) and the graph of your mean latency results.

PROJECT 18

IS THERE A NAZI PERSONALITY?

TONI L. WELCH, DREXEL UNIVERSITY
ERIC A. ZILLMER, DREXEL UNIVERSITY

Personality tests are designed to identify some stable characteristics of a person. For example, is the person outgoing, reliable, sanguine or phlegmatic? In some instances personality assessment is used to determine unusual, inappropriate, or abnormal behavior. Because it is difficult to find independent measures of personality, validating these various tests has been problematic. There are two broad classes of personality tests. One class is the actuarial or structured personality inventory such as the **Minnesota Multiphasic Personality Inventory**, or **MMPI**; the other class is the projective or unstructured test such as the **Rorschach** inkblots. Both these tests were originally validated against clinical populations, such as schizophrenics, and not against normal subjects.

Personality assessment is an important asset to **clinical psychologists** who work in the field of abnormal psychology and in the treatment of mental disorders. Such tests can identify the nature and severity of maladaptive, abnormal, and bizarre behavior patterns as well as facilitate understanding of the conditions that cause or maintain such behaviors. A mental disorder is a psychological state that can be characterized as having dysfunctional, distressful, or disabling impacts in one or more areas of individual functioning. For example, the MMPI has a paranoia scale among others. When a person taking the inventory endorses a number of statements that have factor loadings for paranoia, his or her scale score will be sufficiently elevated that the psychologist might suspect a clinically significant condition. But an MMPI or

Rorschach test by itself is not sufficient as the basis for making a diagnosis, say, of schizophrenia or a related psychotic disorder.

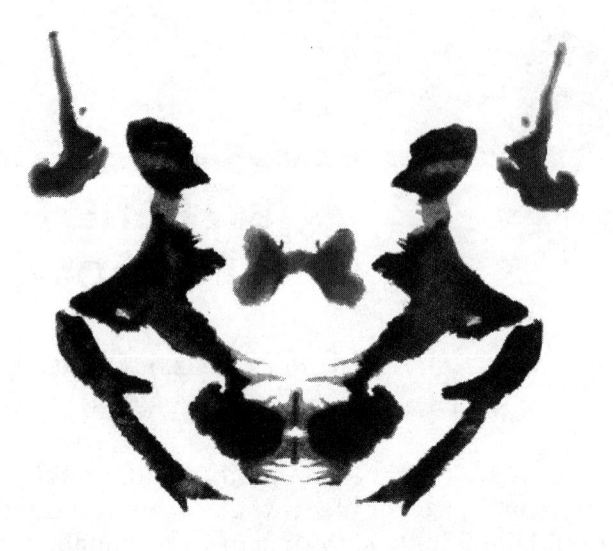

In North America, perhaps the most widely used diagnostic guideline is the American Psychiatric Association's *Diagnostic and Statistical Manual of Mental Disorders*. The **DSM-IV**, the 4th edition, identifies the specific criteria used to establish a particular diagnosis. The DSM includes classifications for sexual disorders, personality disorders, anxiety disorders, psychoactive substance abuse disorders, delusional disorders, and schizophrenia, to name a few. The DSM-IV also provides important resource information such as known predisposing factors, familial patterns, the course and age of onset for each disorder, as well as a glossary of relevant terms.

In this project you will use a biography and selected Rorschach responses of the Nazi war criminal Hermann Goering to conduct a clinical evaluation to determine whether Goering had a **delusional disorder** or **schizophrenia**. Your software contains the stack Goering, A Case Study. In it is Goering's biography and his Rorschach responses from a psychiatric interview conducted shortly after World War II. The stack contains components from the *MacLaboratory for Psychology: Psychological Disorders* package, specifically the DSM Criteria for Delusional Disorders and Schizophrenia and the Psychotic Disorders decision tree. Through them, you may arrive at a diagnosis or at no diagnosis. Based on

Is There A Nazi Personality?

Goering's Rorschach, do you think the Nazis were "beasts" when they did what they did? Or were they human beings? Is evil done by evil men and women, or by ordinary people responding not to malevolent drives within themselves, but to evil situations? It may be that there is no unique "Nazi personality" or that "normal" people are capable of heinous crimes. Why do you suppose some people think that Goering must have been unbalanced, a psychotic killer?

1. PURPOSES

To provide an example of the use and scoring of a Rorschach test. To demonstrate the use of DSM Criteria and the Psychotic Disorders decision tree. To consider the social and cultural forces surrounding psychological diagnosis.

2. APPARATUS

A Macintosh computer with the HyperCard stack Goering, A Case Study. You may also find the stack Personality & Social useful as well as the QuickTime movie *Goering at Nuremberg*. In this project the exact form of your scoring and data collection are left up to you. In all probability, you will want to create a table in Excel or some similar tool.

Goering, A Case Study

Microsoft Excel

3. PROCEDURE

Review the Goering case study provided in the stack.

3.1

Use the following sample scoring strategy to interpret the Rorschach responses. There are 10 summaries of Goering's responses here and at the end of the case study, one for each Rorschach card.

Card I: A funny beetle, a bat, a night animal.
Card II: These are two dancing figures . . . clapping hands.
Card III: 1. Two caricature figures. . . . They are debating over something . . . maybe two doctors arguing over the inner organs of a man (laughs).
          2. You might also say that it is an opened figure of a man.
Card IV: Funny animal, sea animal.

Card V: Night animal... a flying animal... it is more like a bat... the dark color is important.
Card VI: Hide of an animal... here are the legs and backbone. I can see it lying on the floor right in front of me.
Card VII: A face... grotesque... half-man, half-animal.
Card VIII: Two animals climbing up... fantastic sea plants.
Card IX: Very fantastic plant... There are the trolls from Peer Gynt.
Card X: Two crab-like animals. Two troll figures... little dogs Grotesque caricatures... not really alive.

Each statement should be scored, either 0 or 1, for three distinct scales: **Morbidity**, **Fantasy**, and **Conflict**. The criterion receives a 0 if it is not present and a 1 if it is present. Comments that state or suggest death, dying, the termination of existence, or a similar notion should receive a 1 on the Morbidity scale, for example. Comments that indicate persons or events that are magical in nature (e.g., fairies, Superman) should be scored a 1 on the Fantasy scale. Comments that indicate conflict, such as fighting or arguing, unrest, or a state of ensuing conflict should be scored a 1 on the Conflict scale. Calculate the total score. Scores range from 0 to 30, up to 3 points per card for 10 cards. Use your judgment to determine at what point a score is unusual or abnormal.

As a matter of general interest, other scales are also used for scoring the Rorschach, including **Location**, **Determinants**, and **Content** (compare Exner, 1986). Location concerns the portion of the blot that is used—for example, the whole blot, a large detail, or a small detail. Determinants are generally physical factors that are used, such as the color, shape, or shading of a blot. If motion is expressed, then the apparent movement is also a determinant. Content includes the objects the subject reports; these are often human figures or their parts, animals, plants, and sometimes blood.

3.2

Based on the information provided in the case study and the score on the sample interpretation strategy for the Rorschach, determine if Hermann Goering had a psychotic disorder or some other abnormal condition. Provide a complete written exposition of the logic processes you worked through in arriving at your clinical judgment. Indicate how you used the DSM Criteria and the Psychotic Disorders decision tree, including each choice you made. Also include a printout of your Excel table for Rorschach scoring and a brief interpretation of it.

4. Interpretation

The following questions are for discussion, study, and review.

A. Define the following terms and concepts: psychotic disorders, DSM-IV, personality assessment, psychological testing, MMPI, Rorschach, projective tests, structured inventory, schizophrenia, delusional disorder, reliability, validity.

B. Distinguish between psychodynamic, social learning, and trait theories of personality.

C. What is "personality assessment"? What amount, quality, or type of information is provided to the clinician through these measures? How useful do you perceive this information to be? Explain your rational.

D. What are the benefits and drawbacks of having an instrument like the DSM-IV?

E. If you collected class data on your Rorschach scoring, you could do a **split test reliability** by calculating a Spearman rank-order correlation (see Project 9) between the even-numbered cards and the odd-numbered cards. How well do the two halves correlate? What does that mean?

F. How is information obtained to make a diagnosis of mental illness? What is the most effective and reliable means of collecting this information? If you were a clinical psychologist needing to make diagnoses, what would you use, or want to use, to help you make your determination?

G. When using the sample interpretation strategy for the Rorschach, do you feel Goering's score is normal or abnormal? Why?

5. REFERENCES

Exner, J. E. *The Rorschach: A comprehensive system*. Vol. 1. 2d edition. New York: John Wiley, 1986.

Graham, J. *MMPI-2: Assessing personality and psychopathology*. New York: Oxford University Press, 1990.

Irving, D. *Goering: A Biography*. New York: William Morrow, 1989.

Overy, R. J. *Goering: The Iron Man*. London and New York: Routledge & Kegan Paul, 1984.

Zillmer, E., Archer, R., and Castino, R. (1989). Rorschach records of Nazi war criminals: A reanalysis using current scoring and interpretation practices. *Journal of Personality Assessment, 51* (1), 85–99.

Hermann Goering's psychiatric history courtesy of Dr. Eric Zillmer of Drexel University's Neuropsychology Program.

Is There A Nazi Personality? 281

Student _____ Section _____ Due Date _____

IS THERE A NAZI PERSONALITY?

1. Provide a complete written exposition of the logic processes you worked through in arriving at your clinical judgment about Hermann Goering.

2. What is your impression of the Nuremberg movie clip?

3. Provide your interpretation of Goering's Rorschach test.

4. Include any additional material your instructor may require.

5. Attach printouts of your spreadsheets (or hand-scored tables).

PROJECT 19

MEASURING PERSONALITY: TYPE A OR B

LAUREN M. MONTENEGRO
DREXEL UNIVERSITY

The Personality Type A/B questionnaire that comes as a HyperCard stack with your software is a shortened, student-modified form of the Jenkins Activity Survey. This survey was originally formulated to detect the risk of coronary-prone behavior (Jenkins, Zyzanski, & Rosenman, 1971; Robinson, 1988), but the simplified version here cannot be used in that way.

Are you hard-driving and competitive? Do you expect a great deal of yourself with respect to your overall performance—for example, grades in school, performance at work, or ability in sports? If you answered yes to these questions, you tend to have qualities of the Type A personality (Friedman & Rosenman, 1974). Type As are hard workers who are often preoccupied with schedules and the speed of their performance. A study performed by Morell and Katkin (1982) found that professional women had more characteristics of the Type A personality than did homemakers. They were more impatient, hard-driving, and competitive. Consequently, Type As may have a difficult time relaxing. Type B personalities may be more creative, imaginative, and philosophical. They may also be more slothful, indolent, and lazy.

Experiencing high levels of stress for long periods with no time out for relaxation can eventually lead to hypertension and other cardiovascular problems (Jenkins, Rosenman, & Zyzanski, 1974). Hicks, Cheers, and Juarez (1985) found that Type As are generally more susceptible to stress-linked diseases because of the various pressures they place on themselves. Research shows that Type B personalities, however, usually do not pressure themselves. Thus, Type As are prone to feel frustrated and hostile whereas Type Bs are generally relaxed and easy-going.

1. PURPOSES

To challenge the individual student and the class to prepare their own descriptive statistics and public presentation from the personality profile sample of our Type A/B inventory. To role-play a personnel manager in a corporation.

2. APPARATUS

A Macintosh computer with the HyperCard stack Personality Type A/B. This stack contains 20 multiple-choice items and one personal rating scale in a questionnaire format that asks you about your everyday activities and behavior. As with many personality questionnaires, you may not find a response that you feel is exactly right for each item. However, for this example of a structured, forced choice personality inventory, choose the response for each question that best fits your behavior patterns. A total score will be tabulated automatically by an Excel macro or you can hand-score your responses. These scores will also provide data for class analysis. To complete the project, you will need a painting, drawing, or presentation package to create either an electronic data summary or one in print format.

3. Procedure

Open the Personality Type A/B stack. Save your copy in a suitable place and under a suitable name. When you are finished with the questionnaire, click on the Report button in the palette. This will save a text file of your responses. Provide a suitable name for it. After you Quit, open the Excel macro Individual A/B Scoring and read in your individual text file. Save its report.

To collect class data, students should put their files in a common folder designated by your instructor. Running the Excel macro Group A/B Scoring automatically imports class data and produces a class report. If your data are not in the designated folder, they will not be included. Instructors from other sections may pool their data with yours.

Your instructor may wish, or require, you to hand-score your individual results and to calculate your own class data. For this, use an appropriate table of your own or perhaps one from the IRP section of the laboratory manual. Table 19-1 shows the various weightings assigned to the responses for each question.

Basically, if your scores are 2 or more standard deviations above the class mean, you might suspect that you have a Type A personality profile. Students with Type B characteristics are likely to be those whose scores are 2 or more standard deviations below the class mean. *Warning: Don't really label yourself as one personality type or another since the class sample taken was relatively small.* Ideally, you would probably not want to be either a Type A or a Type B personality. Type Bs could miss out on life's opportunities by not setting goals and not taking things seriously enough. Type As could miss out on life's enjoyment unless they learn to relax and take time out for fun.

4. Designing a Data Summary and Presentation

The purpose of this exercise is to apply some of the descriptive statistical concepts you learned from earlier sections of this manual. You will use them to prepare the graphics for a presentation that might represent the sort of brief report you would give as a 5-minute summary and slide show at a company meeting. For example, you could assume you are a personnel manager or an **industrial organizational psychologist** working for the company, and are showing the CEO the results. Use a painting, drawing, or presentation package to create an appropriate number of "slides" or "overheads" for your presentation. Think of your class data as the personality scores from a pool of applicants. Use your own personal data as if they represented a person who was one of the final candidates for the position. Using whatever else you think relevant, give an *objective* appraisal of the candidate on the A/B dimension, what that might mean, and how the candidate compares to the group of candidates as a whole.

Statistics is the science of compacting data so that a few numbers can represent the whole. The purpose is not to "lie" with them but to provide a fair and even-handed summary. Two general classes of **descriptive statistics** are **measures of central tendency** and **measures of variability**. When should you use each of the three measures of central tendency: the **mean**, **median**, and **mode**? Which are appropriate for your report?

The mean is usually the measure of choice. It gives us the best summarized estimate of the center, or fulcrum if you will, of the original group of scores. Yet the mean should be used only when sampling is random and the data approximate the form of a normal curve. The normal curve is symmetrical, with the most common scores plotted in the center and the less common scores creating tails to the sides. Many personality measures are normally distributed, with the average person scoring toward the center of the plot and the more unique person scoring toward one or another of the tails. Sets of scores (perhaps your class data) that are not normally distributed cause the mean to be unrepresentative of the sample taken. For instance, your small company may have five employees, with the president making $100,000 per year and four workers making $25,000 each. The mean of $40,000 is not a good estimate of the average salary. In this case, the mode might better represent the true central tendency. In most cases of **ratio data**, the mode is not reported because the most frequently occurring number may lie at the tail of a distribution. If information is in the form of **nominal data**, however, the mode is the most appropriate. For example, what is the central tendency of automobile makes in your neighborhood? The median is not influenced by extreme scores, so it is a good measure to use when there are scattered data points, resulting in an unrepresentative mean. In the case of a normal curve, all three measures of central tendency should be nearly the same number. The larger the sample size, the more representative these scores.

There are two main measures of variability. These measures tell us how the scores in the data set vary from one another. One measure of variability is the **range**. This is the difference between the highest and lowest scores obtained. The range is quick and easy to tabulate, but it is often unstable because one additional score in the data set could change its value. A better, more frequently used measure of variability is the **standard deviation**. This measure helps us figure out where a given score lies along the normal distribution. By knowing the standard deviation, we can figure out how far a score is from the mean. In presentations, say of a bar graph comparison between two groups, it is common to indicate the standard deviation as a measure of variability about the mean. Your instructor will show you a few of the typical conventions.

Your instructor may also show you a computational formula that has been algebraically rearranged to make calculation of the standard deviation easier. In fact, previous projects have intentionally used a conceptual formula designed to let the less experienced student recognize that the standard deviation is itself an average or mean of differences. For sample sizes less than 60, we typically provide a continuity correction—dividing by $N - 1$ instead of N in calculating the standard deviation of a sample.

Once you know the mean and the standard deviation of a group of scores, you can convert anyone's score into a standard score, which shows where that score fits onto the normal curve. This standard score is called the **z-score** and is tabulated by subtracting the sample mean from the individual's obtained score and dividing that number by the sample standard deviation. The advantage of a z-score is that you can look it up in a statistical table and provide a more familiar measure like a **percentile**. You probably should have a fairly large sample.

Another type of descriptive statistic is a **correlation**. In previous projects we calculated a **nonparametric** correlation, the Spearman rank-order correlation. In this project, if your classmates are willing, you could correlate grades and Type A/B personality scores. Correlation does not prove causality, but it can allow us to make quite accurate predictions.

5. Interpretation

The following questions are for discussion, study, and review.

A. Define descriptive statistics in your own words. Why are these measures important? Name three variables relevant to a personnel department's concerns that are normally distributed.

B. Prior to filling out the questionnaire, did you think you would have more characteristics of the Type A or the Type B personality? Had you filled out the questionnaire without knowing what personality traits it was measuring, do you think your score would have been different? What is the **Rosenthal effect**?

C. Which measure of central tendency best represents the class data? Why? Do you think the mean would change drastically if there were more students in your class?

D. Find the mean, median, and mode for the following set of numbers:

$$2 \quad 3 \quad 5 \quad 5 \quad 5 \quad 10 \quad 10 \quad 15 \quad 20 \quad 25$$

Which measure of central tendency is most representative for this data set? Why?

E. How do you think the format of a personality test affects the psychologist's interpretation? Is the multiple-choice format an effective way for a psychologist to measure behavior? Why or why not?

F. Assuming you are the personnel director, where do you think a good employee should be on the A/B dimension? What types of work would make you take a different point of view? Suppose you were in the company medical department? Is it possible to have too much motivation? What is the **Yerkes-Dodson effect**?

G. Discuss the nature/nurture controversy with respect to either personality or intelligence. Find at least one journal article that argues for nature and one that argues for nurture. Which do you believe plays a larger role in a person's behavior or level of displayed intelligence?

6. REFERENCES

Friedman, M. and Rosenman, R. *Type A Behavior and Your Heart.* New York: Knopf, 1974.

Hicks, R. A., Cheers, Y., and Juarez, M. (1985). Stomach disorders and type A-B behavior. *Psychological Reports, 57,* 1251.

Jenkins, C. D., Rosenman, R. H., and Zyzanski, S. J. (1974). Prediction of clinical coronary heart disease by a test for the coronary-prone behavior pattern. *New England Journal of Medicine, 290,* 1271–1275.

Jenkins, C. D., Zyzanski, S. J., and Rosenman, R.H. (1971). Progress toward validation of a computer-scored test for the type A coronary-prone behavior pattern. *Psychosomatic Medicine, 33,* 193–202.

Morell, M. A. & Katkin, E. S. (1982). Jenkins activity survey scores among women of different occupations. *Journal of Consulting and Clinical Psychology, 50,* 588–589.

Robinson, C.M. (1988). Type A coronary-prone behavior pattern and relaxation through the use of skin temperature biofeedback. Unpublished undergraduate thesis. Washington College, Chestertown, MD.

Student _____ Section _____ Due Date _____

MEASURING PERSONALITY: TYPE A OR B

1. Provide your "slides" or "overheads" in a suitable form for your instructor.

2. Include any additional material your instructor may require.

TABLE 19-1

WEIGHTED SCORING FOR PERSONALITY TYPE A/B QUESTIONNAIRE

Question No.	\multicolumn{4}{c|}{Answer Choice Weighted Values}	\multicolumn{2}{c|}{Individual A/B Scores}
	1	2	3	4	Your Answer	Weighted Score
1.	20	10	5		2	10
2.	25	15	5	0	2	15
3.	0	0	0		4	0
4.	15	5	2		2	5
5.	20	10	2		2	10
6.	0	5	15	15	3	15
7.	2	2	5	15	3	5
8.	50	30	2		2	30
9.	70	50	10	5	2	50
10.	0	0	0		1	0
11.	3	5	10	25	3	10
12.	0	0	0		3	0
13.	2	5	10	15	2	5
14.	30	20	10	2	3	10
15.	0	0	0		2	0
16.	3	10	20		2	10
17.	2	10	25		2	10
18.	20	15	10	3	3	10
19.	10	2	5	15	3	5
20.	0	0	0	0	1	0

The score value for each response on each question is weighted based on the degree to which Type A traits are displayed.

Total: 200

PROJECT 20

HOW DO YOU CONDUCT A GOOD SURVEY?

Psychologists are often involved in opinion, attitude, or survey research. A **counseling psychologist**, for example, may have given you a vocational interest test where a large number of occupations are listed and your profile of responses is matched to the patterns of those actually holding a particular kind of job. Increasingly, politicians, businesspeople, journalists, lawyers, and others are finding that various types of polls or surveys help them do their work better. In this project we look at some of the basic techniques and things to watch out for in constructing a survey questionnaire. We also describe in greater detail than earlier the inferential statistic **chi-square**, which is useful in determining if the observed frequency of responses is significantly different from the expected frequency.

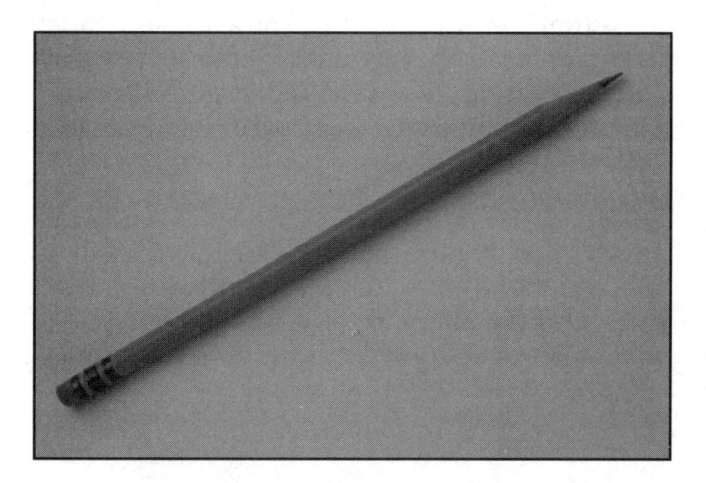

SURVEY CONSTRUCTION

A survey measures behavior and attitudes that exist in a population: an experiment measures certain conditions, often before and after a change imposed by the experimenter. In that sense, surveys are not strictly experiments.

Attitudes are often defined as psychological states involving reason and emotion that predispose people to particular behaviors. Ideally, we would like to examine such psychological states, but in practice we are restricted to measuring behaviors. Thus, attitudes are inferred from observed behaviors, which are in the form of positive and negative statements and actions of varying intensity.

To construct a survey you must first have clearly defined goals and objectives. You must then decide what **population** is to be measured and how you will select your **sample** or contrasting samples. The next step is to design the questionnaire, bearing in mind how you will score your replies and what sort of data analysis you may apply to the results. The questionnaire is normally tried out in pilot form and modified as necessary before data are actually collected. Finally, after analyzing your results, evaluate them in terms of the goals and objectives you initially set out.

SAMPLING STRATEGY

If you wish to be able to generalize from your sample to a defined population, you must choose your sample with extreme care. Simple **random samples** can be used, but they usually need to be quite large to ensure that random representation actually occurs. There are various other sampling strategies. For example, in a **stratified random sample**, specific known characteristics of a population are represented. If you wished to survey engineering majors, a stratified sample would reflect the disproportionate number of males, or minorities, or both, in that population.

QUESTIONNAIRE DESIGN

You will have to decide how many questions you will ask, bearing in mind the amount of data you require, the time available for the survey, and the tolerance of your subjects. As a matter of course, most surveys contain no more than a dozen questions requiring about 10 minutes or less to answer. For more extensive information gathering, say as done by the Gallup Poll, special arrangements with subjects are often required and many times include payment or other rewards for their time.

Any survey should begin with a clear statement of its purpose in order to inform potential subjects. It must conform to **ethical guidelines and standards**. An introduction to any questionnaire should always be presented either verbally or in writing. Where the questionnaire is presented personally, but the subject is asked to fill it out, both an oral introduction and a written introduction should always be given.

If interviewers are used to present the survey, they must be thoroughly conversant with the questionnaire, have answered it themselves, and be competent to answer most of the possible questions arising. The nature of the interviewer's approach is important. All interviewers should be trained under supervision before embarking on solo interviewing.

A survey must always be given in a **standardized** manner; otherwise, differences in a subject's responses may simply be due to the way the material was presented.

Most surveys ask basic **demographic information** such as age that particularly relates to the topic of study. Next follows the main body of the survey. Questions in this portion have often been refined, **scaled**, and ordered as a consequence of pilot research on similar samples. In scaling, independent subjects indicate the "value" of an item and its clarity of meaning. Items normally have a range of scaled values with a reasonably small amount of variability in meaning.

Questions can be **open-ended**, allowing the subjects to express their own views, or **closed-ended**, which means that subjects must choose from the alternatives you supply. Open-ended questions avoid frustration, as the respondents can express their own views, but they are difficult to score. Closed-ended questions are easy to score but may be frustrating unless the options are carefully chosen and cater to all possible views. This means that the response categories must be exhaustive and also mutually exclusive.

Scaled statements may be provided on a questionnaire and attitudes measured on a scale, such as:

Bad taste should be totally banned.

1) Agree strongly
2) Agree
3) No opinion either way
4) Disagree
5) Disagree strongly

Five point scales as above are common, but scales may involve more points or fewer; the number depends on the relevance of the statement and the purpose of the survey. Questionnaires can combine both questions and statements, as this is more flexible and helps maintain respondents' interest.

The authoring tool Survey Master, which comes with *MacLaboratory*, also provides a Visual Scale, a slider where subjects can mark any point along a continuum. This type of scale is convenient if you wish to get at fine gradations in attitudes or are dealing with concepts whose intermediate values are difficult to put into words.

QUESTION EXAMPLES

The following questions from a hypothetical survey of food services at a university illustrate the principles and problems of question construction.

- Items must be clear and unambiguous:

    Cafeteria food is:
    better than elsewhere.
    as good as elsewhere.
    worse than elsewhere.

    Which food? Yesterday's menu or today's? Where is "elsewhere"? Home?

- Avoid double-barreled questions:

    More lockers and coat space should be provided. Agree/Disagree.

    Some people may feel locker space is adequate, but coat space inadequate.

- Your respondent must be competent to answer the question:

    How many times last year did you go to the cafeteria to eat?

    Is this the sort of question that can be answered accurately?

- Questions should be relevant:

    Is the lighting adequate/inadequate in the downstairs coffee bar?

    What of subjects who never entered it?

- Short items are best:

    Many people feel that the principle of having a joint staff and student eating area is of the utmost importance in maintaining harmonious relations on the campus. Do you agree/disagree?

    Long items tend to lead to ambiguity. What is being asked: is it a good idea to have a joint cafeteria or does a joint cafeteria lead to harmonious relations? Understanding and retaining the meaning of long complicated statements is not easy, even when no ambiguities arise.

- Avoid negative items:

    I have never arranged a meal for a university function — Yes/No.

    "Yes" never, or "no" never?

- Avoid biased or loaded items and terms:

    Many students would like to see our rotten food service improved. Wouldn't you?

QUESTION LAYOUT

Try to keep questions well spaced for readability. Underline or italicize key words and phrases. Give clear instructions with examples of how to answer. Do not abbreviate questions. Leave adequate space for answers, including open-ended responses. Clearly label all items and their responses. Arrange a consistent presentation so that responses are clearly associated with their question. Multiple responses to a question generally should be avoided.

Use branching questions to preselect a subgroup of appropriate respondents,

(1) Have you ever eaten on campus? Yes/No
(1.1) If Yes, how many times in the past week? _____

ORDER OF QUESTIONS

The order of questions is often critical to the answers you receive. People usually try to be consistent with earlier responses, so crucial questions should be answered before the respondent is asked for other information on the topic.

ANALYSIS OF RESULTS

Collating and analysis should always be anticipated in the design and layout of the questionnaire as well as in item construction. Many powerful statistical tools for **univariate** and **multivariate** analyses are available.

A useful basic tool for statistical analysis of some types of survey data is **chi-square**. For an example, suppose you have a summer job or a cooperative education placement as a buyer for a local drug store that is part of a national chain. The problem is that expected national demand for products may not match observed local demand. As a marketing major, you know that retail shelf space is expensive, so you want to do a survey and determine if your local demand is **significantly different** from the purchasing recommendations made by the chain.

The chain recommends that you buy equal quantities of three men's hair products: GreaseBall, GoofBall, and WetHead. You conduct a survey for a week and find that total sales are 120, consisting of 40 GreaseBall, 20 GoofBall, and 60 WetHead sales. (It would be a different survey to account for people's tastes!) Are the differences between observed and expected sales significant, or could they be due to chance? Chi-square is calculated as the sum of the squared differences between the observed frequency and the expected frequency, divided by the expected frequency. That sum is compared to a table of critical values at the correct number of degrees of freedom and, if larger, indicates the level of significance. The following figure illustrates the calculation for our problem.

Chi-Square

$$\chi^2 = \Sigma \frac{(Y_i - E_i)^2}{E_i}$$

Y_i = Observed frequency
E_i = Expected frequency

Sample Problem

Class:	Y_i	E_i	$(Y_i - E_i)$	$(Y_i - E_i)^2$	$/E_i$
Greaseball	40	40	0	0	0
Goofball	20	40	−20	400	10
WetHead	60	40	20	400	10
	Σ	120		Σ	20

The results of the calculations show that chi-square = 20. Use Table 20D to determine the level of significance. Look up values based on the **degrees of freedom** ($k - 1$), which, for chi-square, is the number of classes (k)—in this example 3 minus 1, or 2. Since 20 is larger than the critical value of 9.21 (p <.01) you could conclude that local sales probably are differently distributed than national expectations. Therefore, you should devote more shelf space to the WetHead product at the expense of GoofBall.

There are some important things to observe about chi-square. The expected value for any class must always exceed 5. Expected values are estimates based on your **null hypothesis** or some preexisting knowledge of the population. Unlike the sign test, which is a **binomial** test that allows you to compare two classes, Chi-Square is a **Multinomial** test that allows you to compare more than two classes. In our problem, we considered three classes, but there could have been more. Table D provides the critical values of chi-square for a number of degrees of freedom.

TABLE 20D

TABLE OF CRITICAL VALUES FOR CHI-SQUARE

Degrees of Freedom (k – 1)	$\chi^2 = \Sigma \frac{(Y_i - E_i)^2}{E_i}$	
	5% Level	1% Level
1	3.84	6.63
2	5.99	9.21
3	7.81	11.34
4	9.49	13.28
5	11.07	15.09
6	12.59	16.81
7	14.07	18.48
8	15.51	20.09
9	16.92	21.67
10	18.31	23.21
11	19.68	24.72
12	21.03	26.22
13	22.36	27.69
14	23.68	29.14
15	25.00	30.58
16	26.30	32.00
17	27.59	33.41
18	28.87	34.81
19	30.14	36.19
20	31.42	37.57
25	37.65	44.31

How Do You Conduct A Good Survey?

1. Purposes

To use the stack Surveys Master to construct a few examples of survey question types in class. To use chi-square to test an hypothesis about one of the questions the class generates. To complete a course evaluation survey providing feedback to your instructor and to the course, thus aiding their continued improvement.

2. Apparatus

The course evaluation is run on the Macintosh using the stack MacLab Evaluation.

3. Procedure

Use the stack Surveys Master to illustrate different question types. Decide on a survey question or two that will be suitable for using chi-square. Remember the expected value cannot be less than 5 for any class. For example, as a group you might ask:

Which *hair color do most people prefer in the opposite sex?*
( ) *Brown*
( ) *Black*
( ) *Blonde*

The null hypothesis—that there is no preference—would yield an expected frequency of 5 for each class of hair color if there are 15 students. What are the observed student responses? Can the null hypothesis be rejected?

4. Data Analysis

Calculate chi-square for the questions you've generated in class.

5. Interpretation

The following questions are for discussion, study, and review.

A. Define or identify the following: population, sample, stratified sample, null hypothesis, degrees of freedom, multivariate analysis, multinomial, standardized instructions, ethical standards.

B. Could a lawyer use responses to a survey to "stack" a jury in favor of his or her side? What ethical issues does this raise?

C. Can you use chi-square with 1 degree of freedom instead of a sign test?

D. Can media polls cause a change in attitude? Can they affect election results?

E. Why are surveys called "quasi-experimental"?

F. Why are some polls so wrong sometimes?

G. Do people usually tell the truth in surveys?

H. How large is the sample for the Nielsen ratings? Why?

I. What is a semantic differential?

Course Evaluation

1. Please write a brief note describing what you liked best about this course.

2. What were the most important things you learned?

3. Please write a brief note describing what you liked least about this course.

4. Hand in your Course Evaluation stack so your answers can be added to the database. Please make sure there is no identification as we would like your response to be anonymous.

Conclusion

Individual Research Project

CONCLUSION

DESIGN, CREATE, CONDUCT, ANALYZE, AND PRESENT YOUR OWN RESEARCH

1. PURPOSES

To design, create, conduct, and analyze your own research from your proposal in Project 5. To be alert to ethical issues in human research. To introduce a scientific communication style. Your instructor may suggest a poster presentation (Chute & Bank, 1983), a formal journal article, or an electronic "talk" like that which would be given at a scientific convention.

2. APPARATUS

MacLaboratory is, of course, available. You may however, decide to do any ethical and approved experiment, survey, or naturalistic observation. Other apparatus may be requested through your laboratory instructor.

3. PROCEDURES FOR A WRITTEN JOURNAL ARTICLE

Scientific communication benefits from a standardized reporting format. Any journal article in a field presents a model that probably conforms to the following outline. Your experience in this course has already lead you through a **process approach** to accomplishing this goal.

3.1

The purpose of writing a report is to communicate your reasons for doing the experiment, how you did it, the results you obtained, and the conclusions you reached.

3.2

A general fault in writing reports is to use emotive language; this might bias the reader's own conclusions.

3.3

The report is organized:

> *Title*
> *Abstract* (100 words)
> *Introduction*
> *Method*, (containing apparatus, procedure, and subject details)
> *Results* (descriptive and inferential)
> *Discussion*
> *References*
> *Appendix* (as necessary)

3.4

Keep the report as concise and clear as possible.

3.5

The Abstract is a summary of the main points of the Introduction, Method, Results, and Discussion.

3.6

The Introduction contains sufficient background material for the reader to understand why you did the experiment, and it explains the rationale for carrying it out.

3.7

The Method section contains details of subjects, details of apparatus and other materials, and details of general design and other procedural points.

3.8

The Results section contains descriptive statistics (figures and tables) and inferential statistics and tests. A result is described by indicating the difference and direction the descriptive scores take, and the results of the inferential statistical test.

3.9

The discussion section draws your results together, compares them to other experiments particularly referred to in the Introduction, and draws conclusions therefrom.

3.10

References contain details of papers, books, and other publications that have been consulted and are referred to in the text. Cite only material actually consulted.

3.11

The Appendix contains all computational and raw data you drew upon in the paper.

TITLE

The Title should convey in brief the nature of the study, because the title is going to largely determine who reads the report. If the Title is misleading, the people who should read the report may not do so. The Title is also a primary source of information for professional indexers who prepare reference works. Optimally, the Title should be brief but contain all the "key" words that one would ordinarily look for in that field of interest.

ABSTRACT

Purpose: The purpose is a brief summary of your reasons for doing the experiment, how it was done, the results, and your conclusions. It should tell potential readers whether the article's contents would be of interest to them.

Format: The length is traditionally about 100–120 words. The Title is omitted. The general ordering of information follows that of the text.

Faults:

1. Often the Abstract is vague. Be as specific as possible—for example, "8 male subjects aged 20–22 enrolled at Drexel University." Try to introduce key words that convey useful information to the reader.

2. Do not make overgeneralizations, even though you are restricted as to space.

INTRODUCTION

Purpose: The Introduction is usually about a quarter the length of the report. The length reflects its importance. This is the section that describes the broader aspects of the problem you are confronting.

Format: The first part of the Introduction should contain sufficient information on the historical background of the problem for the uninformed reader to see what has already been done, when, and by whom. The historical background should contain a brief description of earlier experiments that are relevant to yours and from which your experiment has been derived. Experiments are usually considered relevant if yours (1) improves on their methodology; (2) uses their technique; (3) qualifies or extends their results; (4) complements their result in another area; (5) contradicts their conclusions; or (6) integrates their conclusions into a more general result or conclusion. The second section of the Introduction is more concerned with your experiment. It should explain how your experiment is going to add to or clarify the earlier results. The reader should be told here, in general terms, what your study proposes to do. Accordingly, the reader should be told what variables will be examined and what hypothesis will be tested. If your experiment uses a theory about behavior, then you will have to specify what aspects of the theory you are testing, and why.

Faults:

1. The most common fault is to write an incomplete Introduction. Although brevity and conciseness are essential, your Introduction should contain sufficient information for a reader to understand why you did the experiment and what conclusions you drew from the literature. If your Introduction is incomplete, you will

find you need to introduce some new background material in the final Discussion. It may be beneficial to you to ask someone else to read the Introduction and comment on how well they understand the reasons for doing the experiment.

2. Specific hypotheses and testable ideas are often not precisely put. It is important both for reader comprehension and for the impact and import of the paper to specify hypotheses in formal terms and with a concise statement of the logic by which one result rather than another is expected.

METHOD

Purpose: The purpose of the Method section is to tell the reader how the study was conducted. The actual mechanisms of the experiment are described. This section should contain enough information to allow someone else to be able to repeat your experiment.

Format: The Method section always contains at least three subsections: Subjects, Apparatus, and Design and Procedure.

Subjects: The Subjects subsection answers three questions about the subjects: Who were they? How many were there? and How were they selected? In describing the subjects, major demographic characteristics such as age, sex, socioeconomic status (and breed or strain, in the case of animals) are reported. You may also need to mention other features relevant to the experiment. You should state the method of selection, which might be random sampling, stratified random sampling, friendship with the experimenter, or whatever. In the case of naturalistic observation studies, be sure to describe the location of and conditions under which your observations occurred and how you identified or classified the animals or humans you observed.

Apparatus: The Apparatus subsection should contain details of the apparatus or material used. You need to describe the general function of a piece of apparatus, as well as its relevant features, such as the sound intensity it might produce, its brightness, or its exposure duration if you are using visual or auditory displays. Often you will be using paper and pencil tests based on written material. Here, you need to specify the relevant features of the written material.

Design and Procedures: Clearly identify the independent, dependent, and controlled variables. Provide the "recipe" you followed in collecting your data.

Faults: The usual fault is providing only a description of the Procedure employed. Although it is necessary for readers to know the details of the experiment, they must also know the design used—the way these details were put together. You need to provide the general description of the design and method before introducing procedural details. Make sure the "recipe" is stated simply, step by step, so anyone can exactly replicate your experiment. Include in detail lengthy materials you used, but place them in an appendix.

Results

Purpose: In the Results section, you present the actual results or findings of the experiment. It is essential that you first present tables and graphs of your basic results in means or percentages, as appropriate. Only then should you present the results of appropriate statistical tests. It is not sufficient simply to give the numbers. The tables, graphs, and statistical tests should be accompanied by a written description of those selected findings that direct the reader's attention to the significant features.

Format: Individual scores of subjects are rarely reported. (If they are, the anonymity and privacy of your subjects must be ensured.) Instead, the results are presented in the form of means, percentages, proportions, or deviations, in tables or graphs, with a brief title including units of measurement. These results appear before the results of statistical tests are presented. Tables and figures are numbered consecutively and separately. Aim to present in a table or figure the data necessary to support one of the important points of the experiment. Accompanying the tables and figures should be a written description of these results with references to appropriate tables or figures (e.g., "As Table 2 shows, males produced more errors than females.") Each point that you try to make in the Results should, if possible, be supported by a statistical test.

Faults: Common faults are:
1. Not providing a verbal description of the findings, including the direction of the difference, in association with the statistical tests.

2. Not providing adequate tables and figures to illustrate the group means, percentages, and so on for the relevant experimental conditions.

3. Failure to give each table and figure a descriptive title.

4. Calling a figure a graph and vice versa.

5. Putting tables and figures in the Appendix rather than in the Results, where they belong.

6. Including details in the text that belong in the Appendix.

7. Creating confusion by not clearly expressing probability levels. There are three common conventions: "$p < .05$" (probability is less than 5 in 100), which is directly equivalent to "p is less than 5%" and "significant at the 5% level."

Discussion

Purpose: In the Results, the fundamental findings of the study are presented. These form the building blocks for the report. The Discussion contains the cement to link these results together and tie them to all the background information presented in the Introduction. The section also often includes suggestions for future research, where appropriate.

Format: Format of the Discussion is fairly flexible. The aim is to draw inferences and conclusions about your data and relate them to theory as necessary. Practical implications of the results are drawn out and discussed in relation to other experiments and findings. Most experiments contain a few unanticipated results. These can be due either to unexpected flaws in the methodology or to unexplored variables. These points should be noted and discussed as deficiencies of the design or as suggestions for future work. The organization of the Discussion usually progresses from the specific findings of the experiment to a more general discussion of all related experiments.

Faults: The main faults are:
1. Presenting material and references that should logically have occurred in the Introduction.

2. Presenting an incomplete interpretation of present results.

3. Presenting the results of other research irrelevant to the point of the present experiment, and that have not been noted in the Introduction.

REFERENCES

Purpose: At the end of the report, you should list all sources of information cited in the text. References are listed alphabetically according to the surname of the author(s). When more than one article by the same author is cited, those articles should be ordered by year of publication. The purpose of references is to enable interested readers to both follow up your work with supplementary reading and to allow evaluation of your work in the light of existing knowledge. Include anything you read that was relevant, but ensure that you cite the reference at some point in the text. Do not include any references you have not actually read.

Bibliographic References

Format: A journal reference is presented as: Author's name (year of publication), title of article, name of journal, volume number, and the first and last pages. Author's name is in upper- and lowercase lettering, and the volume number and journal title are underlined or italicized:

> Wine, J. (1971). Test anxiety and direction of attention. *Psychological Bulletin, 76,* 92–104.

> Chute, D.L. and Bank, B. (1983). Undergraduate seminars: The poster session solution. *Teaching of Psychology, 10* (2), 99–100.

A book reference is presented as: author's name, title of book, city of publication, publisher, year of publication. Author's name is in upper- and lowercase lettering and the book title is underlined or italicized:

> Thorndike, E.L. and Lorge, I. *The teacher's wordbook of 30,000 words.* New York: Columbia University Teachers' College, 1944.

A reference to a publication within a book is presented as: Author's name, title of section, editor's name, book title (underlined or italicized), city of publication, publisher, and year of publication:

> Rachman, S.J. Observational learning and therapeutic modeling. In M.P. Feldman and A. Broadhurst (eds.), *Theoretical and experimental bases of behavior therapies.* London: Wiley, 1976.

Citations in the Text

Format: Citations presented in the text should correspond to references given in the list at the end of the article; be sure spelling and date agree. Format differs slightly according to whether the author's name is literally cited in the text or merely given as a reference. Only surname and year of publication are cited. Note position of parentheses:

> Chute (1988) asserts that the Macintosh can serve as a cognitive prosthesis for neurologically impaired patients.

> The Macintosh can serve as a cognitive prosthesis for neurologically impaired patients (Chute, 1988).

When citing a book in the text, give page numbers also. When citing an article you have not read but that is referred to by another author, the format is:

> Chute (1988, cited by Lynch, 1989) asserts that the Macintosh can serve as a cognitive prosthesis for neurologically impaired patients.

Faults: The main faults are:
1. Inadequate referencing—that is, there are not enough background references provided to complete the reader's knowledge.
2. Citations in the text omitted in the reference list, and vice versa.
3. References of works not actually consulted.

APPENDIX

Because journal articles rarely contain an Appendix, the standards given here depart from usual practice. You normally need to include an appendix in your IRP so your work can be thoroughly evaluated.

Purpose and Format: The kind of information appearing in appendices include mathematical derivations and calculations, calculations for statistical tests that were carried out, individual scores on the experimental tests, samples of experimental material or questionnaires, verbatim instructions, and any other information necessary for the Instructor to form a comprehensive opinion of the work and to check any mistake you might have made.

Faults: Although the work is often "rough copy," carry it out neatly, so it is intelligible.

FINAL WORDS

Stimulus is singular, and *stimuli* is plural. Data *are* plural. Give all dimensions on illustrative figures. Use centimeters, grams, and seconds rather than the Imperial or American system of measurement. As a general rule, do not use other abbreviations except for measurements.

For those who might be interested in the history of this curriculum and software, the following two papers and their references may be of interest:

> Chute, D. L. (1993). MacLaboratory for Psychology: Success, failures, economics, and outcomes over its decade of development. *Behavior Research Methods Instruments and Computers*, 25(2), 180–188.

> Chute, D. L. (1994). The psychology "Classroom 2000" project: A personal view of what the past tells us about the future. *Social Science Computer Review* (in press).

Individual Research Project

Student _____ Section _____ Due Date _____

INDIVIDUAL RESEARCH PROJECT

1. Attach your research report entitled:

INDIVIDUAL RESEARCH PROJECT
Statistical Tables and Worksheets

Sign Test

The sign test is an inferential statistic used when you have two sets of data generated by the same individual. Project 3 includes a discussion of the logic and use of this test. Following, you will find a table of critical values and a sample worksheet.

Mann–Whitney *U*-Test

The Mann–Whitney *U*-test is an inferential statistic used when you have two sets of data generated by different groups of individuals. Project 4 includes a discussion of the logic and use of this test. Following, you will find a table of critical values and a sample worksheet .

Spearman Rank-Order Correlation, (ρ)

The Spearman ρ is a descriptive statistic showing the correlation between two sets of ranked data. Project 9 includes a discussion of the logic and use of this test. Following, you will find a table of critical values and a sample worksheet.

Chi-Square

Chi-square is a parametric inferential statistic used when you have two or more classes of frequency data. Chi-square determines whether the observed frequencies are different from the expected frequencies. Project 20 includes a discussion of the logic and use of this test. Following, you will find a table of critical values and a sample worksheet.

IRP

SIGN TEST OF STATISTICAL SIGNIFICANCE

Sample Size (N) Subtract 1 from N for each tie	Number of plus signs required when the direction of difference is predicted (One-tailed test)	
	5% Level	1% Level
5	5	5
6	6	6
7	7	7
8	8	8
9	9	9
10	10	10
11	11	11
12	12	12
13	13	13
14	14	14
15	15	15
16	16	16
17	17	17
18	18	18
19	19	19
20	20	20
21	21	21
22	22	22
23	23	23
24	24	24
25	25	25

Individual Research Project

IRP

SIGN TEST WORKSHEET

Subject No.			Sign
1.			
2.			
3.			
4.			
5.			
6.			
7.			
8.			
9.			
10.			
11.			
12.			
13.			
14.			
15.			
16.			
17.			
18.			
19.			
20.			
Significance Level $p <$		Total No. of Plus Signs	

IRP

MANN-WHITNEY *U*-TEST OF STATISTICAL SIGNIFICANCE

Sample Size Group A	Sample Size Group B	Constant	5% Level	1% Level
4	4	26	2	0
5	4	30–35*	3	0
5	5	40	4	1
6	5	45–51*	5	2
6	6	57	7	3
7	6	63–70*	9	5
7	7	77	11	6
8	7	84–92*	13	8
8	8	100	16	10
9	8	108–117*	18	11
9	9	126	21	14
10	9	135–145*	24	16
10	10	155	27	19
11	10	165–176*	31	22
11	11	187	34	25
12	11	128–210*	38	28
12	12	222	42	31
13	12	234–247*	47	35
13	13	260	51	39

Subtract the largest sum of ranks from the constant. This result is significant if it is = or < the values below.

* If the largest sum of ranks comes from the largest group, use the larger constant. If the largest sum comes from the smaller group, use the smaller constant.

Individual Research Project

IRP

Mann-Whitney *U*-Test Worksheet

Combined rank	Score	Ranks		
1				Combine the scores from both groups of data and list them in rank order in the Score column.
2				
3				If the score came from the group in the "light gray" Ranks column, enter its rank in that column.
4				
5				If the score came from the group in the "medium gray" Ranks column, enter its rank in that column.
6				
7				If scores are tied, assign an average rank to the appropriate columns.
8				
9				
10				Sum the two Ranks columns, subtract the LARGEST sum from the constant determined by group size in the preceding table and determine the significance level.
11				
12				
13				
14				
15				
16				
17				
18				
19				
20				
Σ				
Significance Level	p			

IRP

CRITICAL VALUES FOR SPEARMAN ρ

Sample Size (N) Number of Paired Scores	Significance level for the absolute value of ρ equal to or greater than the tabled value (Two-tailed test)	
	5% Level	1% Level
5	1.000	
6	.886	1.000
7	.786	.929
8	.715	.881
9	.700	.834
10	.649	.794
11	.619	.764
12	.588	.735
13	.561	.704
14	.539	.680
15	.522	.658
16	.503	.636
17	.488	.618
18	.474	.600
19	.460	.585
20	.447	.570
21	.437	.556
22	.426	.544
23	.417	.532
24	.407	.521
25	.398	.511

Individual Research Project

IRP

SPEARMAN ρ WORKSHEET

Subject No.	Scores		Ranks		D	D^2
1.						
2.						
3.						
4.						
5.						
6.						
7.						
8.						
9.						
10.						
11.						
12.						
13.						
14.						
15.						
16.						
17.						
18.						
19.						
20.						

$$\rho = 1 - \left(\frac{6 \Sigma D^2}{N(N^2 - 1)} \right)$$

Σ

$\rho =$

Significance Level ρ

IRP

TABLE OF CRITICAL VALUES FOR CHI-SQUARE

Degrees of Freedom (k – 1)	$\chi^2 = \Sigma \frac{(Y_i - E_i)^2}{E_i}$	
	5% Level	1% Level
1	3.84	6.63
2	5.99	9.21
3	7.81	11.34
4	9.49	13.28
5	11.07	15.09
6	12.59	16.81
7	14.07	18.48
8	15.51	20.09
9	16.92	21.67
10	18.31	23.21
11	19.68	24.72
12	21.03	26.22
13	22.36	27.69
14	23.68	29.14
15	25.00	30.58
16	26.30	32.00
17	27.59	33.41
18	28.87	34.81
19	30.14	36.19
20	31.42	37.57
25	37.65	44.31

IRP

Chi-Square Worksheet

Chi-Square				
$\chi^2 = \Sigma \dfrac{(Y_i - E_i)^2}{E_i}$			Y_i = Observed frequency E_i = Expected frequency	

Class df = k − 1	Y_i	E_i	$(Y_i - E_i)$	$(Y_i - E_i)^2$	$/E_i$
Conflict	25.4	24.65	.75	.5625	.023
Non Conflict	23.9	24.65	−.75	.5625	.023
				Σ	.046